CONTENTS

INTERNATIONAL MAGAZINE OF AUTOMOBILES AND OTHER OBJETS D'ART

N° 3 - SEPTEMBER 1992

Chief Editor
Roberto Merlo

Deputy Editor
Giancarlo Mariani

Contributors at
Ettore Bugatti S.r.l. and
Bugatti Automobili S.p.a.
Ivo Ceci
(Historical archive)
Daniela Kettmeir
(Cultural centre)
Sabrina Nacca
(Press office)
Barbara Pindilli
(Editorial secretary)

Graphic design
and Typesetting
Romano Vitale
(Studio Tabloid)

Translations
Neil Davenport
(English)
Marie Paule Duverne
(French)
Patrick Fael
(German)

Contributors to this issue
Romano Artioli
Marco Bellucci
Giampaolo Benedini
Enrico Benzing
Jean-Marc Borel
Armido Cavalca
Ivo Ceci
Giuseppe Maghenzani
Mario Merlo
Gianni Sighinolfi
Giorgio Terruzzi
Jean Philippe Vittecoq

Photographs
Agence Gamma
Bugatti Archives
Museo dell'Automobile
Carlo Biscaretti
di Ruffia Archives
Sandro Bacchi (cover)
Angelo Bianchetti
Roberto Bigano
Roberto Carrer
Claudio Colombo
Umberto Guizzardi
Gianni Sighinolfi

GIORGIO NADA EDITORE

Head Office, administrative
and editorial office
via Claudio Treves, 15/17
20090 Vimodrone Mi
tel. 02/27301126 -
fax 02/27301454

Editorial coordination
Daniele Antonietti

Co-editor in Great Britain
for the English language edition
Veloce Publishing
Godmanstone - Dorset DT2 7AE
tel. 0300/341602 - fax 0300/341065

Co-editor in France
for the French language edition
E.P.A.
9-13, Rue du Colonel Pierre Avia
BP 501 75725 Parigi
tel. 01/46429191 - fax 01/47369465

Co-editor in Germany
for the German language edition
Heel Verlag
Hauptstrasse 354
5330 Königswinter 1
tel. 02223/23027 - fax 02223/23028

Distributors
ITALIA
Giovanni De Vecchi Editore
via Vittor Pisani, 16
20124 Milano

GIAPPONE
Hokuto Corporation
32-5 Minamidai 3-chome
Nakano-ku
Tokyo 164

OLANDA
Meko Books
Wilhelminastraat 15
2011 VH Haarlem

STATI UNITI
Motorbooks International
729 Prospect Avenue
Osceola Wisconsin 54020

Mail order sales
Libreria dell'Automobile
corso Venezia, 43
20121 Milano
tel. 02/27301462-27301468
fax 02/27301454

Registration
at the Milan court
n. 188 del 21/3/1992

Photocomposition
Studio Tabloid, Milan

Photolithography
Fotolito Mazzucchelli, Milan

Printed by
Grafiche Mazzucchelli, Milan

Advertising
Giorgio Nada Editore
(Aldo Ghirardi)
via Claudio Treves 15/17
20090 Vimodrone
tel. 02/27301126 R.A.
fax 02/27301454

EDITORIAL

« *W hen an objective is reached — Ettore Bugatti liked to say — you must never stop and rest on your laurels. This is only the starting point for the conquest of new horizons.*» *It was a maxim that the great automobile pioneer, together with his collaborators, applied to all aspects of his life, including his work. The same philosophy is followed at Bugatti today, just as in the past.*
The targets are achieved, one after the other, but the company continues to look to the future in a search for new challenges.
In just three years Bugatti has succeeded in constructing an industrial reality unique in its field and to produce a masterpiece of a car. In its first six months the EB 110 has overcome all of the severest type approval tests. With the 342 km/h recorded during the demanding tests on the Nardò ring it has also demonstrated that it is the world's fastest series-built Gran Turismo.
The Campogalliano assembly lines are now working flat out to guarantee delivery of the cars to the first fortunate owners, according to the previously arranged timetable. The company's most immediate commercial objective concerns the formation and development of a network of concessionaires on a par with the standard of the product and coherent with the Bugatti image. The EB 110's competition programme will then be defined and ambitious new projects will see the light of day. Our publishing company has also wished to follow Ettore Bugatti's philosophy. We have not rested on our laurels either, but have continued to progress, improving the contents and quality of the magazine. The third issue has more pages and is rich in exclusive features dedicated to style, technology, culture and news. Without forgetting the vital contribution made by men responsible for the renaissance of the Bugatti dream.

GENEVA: THE WORLD'S AUTOMOTIVE MECCA

The world-wide consecration of the new Bugatti at the industry's most important exposition. The show-goers take the two EB 110s by storm.

BY ROMANO ARTIOLI

The greatest attraction at the 1992 Geneva Show, the world's most important, was undoubtedly the Bugatti EB 110. The car had already been presented at the Bologna Motor Show in the presence of the Italian public where it had enjoyed a remarkable success.

Geneva was the car's first outing at an international motor show, and so you can imagine how we felt at having to measure ourselves against all the world's car manufacturers and to undergo the critical examination of all the specialists who traditionally gather at the Swiss show to exchange impressions of latest novelties offered by the automotive industry.

Pulses were beating faster because we had decided to present a new version of the

→

Above, the
extremely
crowded Bugatti
stand which
was the
true centre of
the Swiss show.
On the facing
page, the
EB 110 S.

EB 110, the Supersport, and as those in the industry well know, these novelties always end up being finished off just a few minutes before the presentation.

The tension lasted until the trucks carrying the cars arrived in the car-park of the Palaexpò. There was a handshake from Giancarlo Vettori who, as ever, along with his men took care of every last detail of the exposition, and a brief comment on what there was to be done for the forthcoming Paris exposition, then the great success, an uninterrupted queue of journalists who throughout the two press days thronged the stand to pick up their press packs. We received compliments from our great neighbours who discovered that the Bugatti project was useful in maintaining a high profile for European products. A necessary and two-way profile, but one that will never penalize or be competitive because Bugatti's very nature means that it will never invade the fields of the other manufacturers: its technical contents will always set it apart and its products will always be built in very limited numbers whatever the future market developments.

EB

The best was yet to come, that is to say the Geneva public who are normally composed and patient, but in order to see the Bugatti thronged and jammed the corridors around our stand.

It was often necessary, especially at the weekend, to call in the hall's security men to save women and children from the crush and to regulate the flow of people fascinated by the two cars, the blue Gran Turismo and the silver Supersport, which rotated continuously on turntables.

We had considerable difficulties ourselves

On the rotating platform, under the spotlights, the highly acclaimed star of Geneva: the Supersport version of the EB 110.

trying to get through the masses swarming around, and it got to the point where we had to sacrifice a few shirt buttons in order to reach the stand. Aside from these problems, which did not worry us too much however as we had the honour of having far and away the best attended stand at the show, we received many comments that made all our work worthwhile... "At last, cars that break with the old traditions and offer avant-garde technical contents..." ..."It is the smallest, most compact of today's GTs..." ..."I never thought that the EB 110 would be flanked by a new version in such a short space of time... and what a Supersport!" ..."It's much more beautiful than in the photographs." ..."There are marques at the show which have presented more expensive cars with inferior contents..." "I don't know which of the two to choose, they're both very attractive." ..."Bugatti is truly the Number One in the Gran Turismo sector."

Then along came the droves of engineers, designers and stylists who, of course, all wanted to see and discover every last detail of the cars. Sabrina Nacca, Donata Gianesi and Anja Wartenberg, entrusted with the Public Relations side, worked flat out to answer all the questions on the small but refined stand designed by the architect Benedini and prepared to show our cars at their best.

Given the public success that we found, we will be back again next year. We hope that the organizers will do something to allow an orderly flow around our stand which will again be a point of reference because there will again be a new Bugatti at the centre of attention.

It was all enormously tiring, from start to finish, but to enter the hall and see the Bugatti name once again hung among the other celebrated marques was just so gratifying that the fatigue and tension melted away and were immediately replaced by joy and satisfaction. ☐

The Chairman, Romano Artioli, explains to Clay Regazzoni the specification of the new Campogalliano Gran Turismo.

Luca di Montezemolo, Chairman of Ferrari, visiting the Bugatti stand, stopped to talk with Romano Artioli.

The dynamic Bugatti Public Relations officer, Sabrina Nacca, with one of the illustrious guests, ingegnere Mauro Forghieri.

The three-time Formula 1 World Champion, the Scotsman Jackie Stewart meets the Bugatti Chairman at Geneva.

THE EVOLUTION
OF THE SPECIES

*More powerful, faster, lighter.
The EB 110 S is characterized by new air
intakes, alloy wheels of a brand-new
design and a fixed wing. The simple, spare
interior has a decidedly racy air.*

BY GIAMPAOLO BENEDINI

The Gran Turismos enjoyed their heyday at the end of the Fifties and into the Sixties. Destined for use as touring machines but blessed with excellent high speed performance, these cars were often used by amateur drivers in sporting events which, at that time, were much less aggressively competitive than they are now. Nowadays, for various reasons, there are no cars that can be used *sic et simpliciter* in daily traffic and in competition. Safety norms, regulations and tyres differentiate the two conditions of use which generally require different specifications for the cars. The EB 110 is a true Gran Turismo, capable of reaching three hundred and forty-two km/h (!), but also extremely docile.

The car is a perfect blend of performance, flexibility and quiet running, equipped with accessories and produced with interior materials and forms that provide sensations of reassuring comfort. It is the result of a precise product philosophy in complete opposition to those who would like to see these cars relegated to collectors' garages. The performance figures homologated by the EB 110 currently represent the absolute peak

continues on page 12

In the two overhead views the EB 110 S shows off its strongly sporting personality. The aggressiveness of the styling is underlined, especially at the rear, by the large new NACA-type air intakes on the rear screen.

continues from page 9

in the supercar field, yet this is still a car that is easily tamed; it is thus very usable and it will not be rare to see members of the fairer sex behind the wheel of the new Bugatti.

ℨ

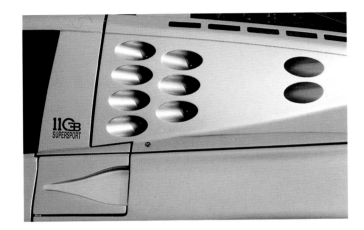

Among car enthusiasts exists a hardened band of devotees of the ultimate in high speed performance; for the sake of ever more intense sensations they are quite prepared to renounce certain accessories and put up with more noise.

The Supersport version, an EB 110 in practically track-ready form, has been created to satisfy these extremists. Power output has been increased (600 hp), and the radio, air conditioner and electric windows have been struck off the standard equipment list. Quick release catches keep the bonnet and engine cover in place thus eliminating the linkages necessary for opening the covers from the cockpit. The bon-

net and engine cover themselves are made from carbonfibre; the bonnet is the same shape as that of the EB 110, whilst the rear cover has been produced with a fixed wing (thus eliminating the servos controlling the movement of EB 110's wing) and new air intakes to cope with more extreme use.

The wheels are of a new design (again produced in collaboration with BBS) allowing the greater brake ventilation necessary in the case of continuous use on the track. The interior, which is still trimmed in leather of the highest quality, has been revised with function and high performance in mind: a weight paring operation involving the steering wheel, seats (with an anatomical shell in carbonfibre), simplified door panels, the woodwork, the instrument binnacle and the sound deadening materials has been carried out. The result is ex-

tremely sporting without renouncing an image of exclusive product quality. The glass side windows and rear screen have been replaced by lighter and indestructible polycarbonate items.

All these visible and hidden modifications (much of the weight saving concerns the engine and the chassis) have resulted in an overall saving of 200 kg and have given the car an extremely aggressive and sporting image.

It is a machine destined for those looking for even more direct and emotive involvement at the wheel of a Bugatti, where the rapport between car and driver is even more immediate. The Supersport, presented at Geneva, has divided the Bugatti fans into two factions and has brought the marque closer to other enthusiasts. On the other hand we could hardly forget the thousands of victories which contributed to the creation of the legend: the EB 110 Supersport is dedicated to all competition enthusiasts. □

TEN SOLOISTS
FOR A CONCERTO

*Behind the scenes of the EB 110
project with the men
of the Bugatti technical team.
Experience, understanding
and environment are the secrets
of their success*

BY ROBERTO MERLO

The legendary live performances of the
most famous chamber orchestras such
as "I Virtuosi di Roma", the English Chamber Orchestra, the Prague Soloists or the
Academy of St. Martin in the Fields have
three small-but-important secrets in common. The first lies in the experience and
ability of the single musicians who, renouncing individualism, play not for themselves
but in relation to the collective performance.

→

In the large photo, the engineers with their creation. From the left: Fernando Gabellini, Luciano Caruso, Giampaolo Benedini, Federico Trombi, Pavel Rajmis, Nicola Materazzi, Tiziano Benedetti, Stefano Mion, Achille Bevini and Oliviero Pedrazzi. Alongside, Ettore Bugatti, with drivers and collaborators, behind the 1930 type 46 chassis.

The second concerns the great understanding reached by the musicians after constant practice together. Lastly, the third secret is linked to the environment which has to be acoustically perfect to exalt the intensity and harmony of the sound. If just one of the elements of this cocktail is lacking the orchestra is no longer perfect and even the execution of a piece of baroque music may seem dense and colourless.

The comparison might seem a little far-fetched but, as in the case of the chamber orchestras, at Bugatti too experience, understanding and environment are the key factors which have allowed the Campogalliano technical team to produce an engineering and styling masterpiece like the EB 110. The men behind the design of the new Gran Turismo are few in number. Ten engineers of great talent and professionalism who, in just three years, have brought a dream to life. Giampaolo Benedini, vice-chairman of the company and head of the Styling Centre,

was the designer of the whole Campogalliano complex. In the design of the new works, in harmony with the criteria applied by Ettore Bugatti himself, the traditional layouts typical of industrial architecture were ignored. "The primary objective — professes Bendini — was that of looking after the personnel, putting them into as light an environment as possible, in contact with the exterior and in favourable climatic conditions, so that they wouldn't feel as though they were shut into a cage. There are few factories which satisfy these criteria." Campogalliano is the fruit of a global project which involved all aspects of the environment: from the assembly lines to the chairman's office furniture, from the draughtsmen's drawing boards to the employees, clothing. This has contributed to the creation of an *esprit de corps* by providing a unified, coordinated image. The men of the Bugatti team have been chosen not only on the basis of their professionalism and experience, but also in relation to certain human factors. Nicola Materazzi, Bugatti technical director, had the by no means easy task of identifying the right people for the

EB 110 project. A design engineer of great talent, *ingegnere* Materazzi has worked at Lancia, Abarth, Osella and Ferrari. At the latter he directed the racing department's technical office and after having moved over to the series production side was involved in the development of the 288 GTO, the

Testarossa, the 208 Turbo, the 328, the 412 and the F 40. "At Bugatti, he says, people with notable backgrounds have come together, often arriving from other car makers. In many cases I made personal contact with those engineers I felt were best suited to perform a particular task within the firm. The choice fell on men with excellent professional backgrounds but who above all were willing to work as a team. In the past the design of a car was developed by just one person who was able to more or less harmonize all the various elements.

Today, with the increase in the number of variables, the problem is far more complex. The production of a new vehicle is always the fruit of the coordinated work or a number of individuals who have to find together a satisfactory compromise, the ideal balance among the various components."

Ingegnere Luciano Caruso from Siracusa, the technical vice-chairman, joined Bugatti

at the end of last year after a long career at the Fiat research centre, the Ferrari racing department (as an engineer) and at Alfa Romeo where he was involved in the Indy sports programme. "The dynamic spirit of competition — says Caruso — and the inevitable team-work which derives from it can certainly be transferred to the world of series production, with undeniable advantages from the technical and human points of view. On the occasion of the homologation tests at Nardò we gave a clear demonstration of the validity of this method." A con-

siderable number of engineers from the Emilia region work at Bugatti. Men who are creative by nature, almost protagonists in the work in which they are involved. At Campogalliano, where the contribution made by each individual is of vital importance, an Emilian can find an ideal environment in which to develop his professional skills. In fact the "historic" nucleus of designers is composed of Tiziano Benedetti, Achille Bevini and Oliviero Pedrazzi, all from Modena. Three truly creative engineers who be-

→

In the large photo, the technical director, Nicola Materazzi. Top, Romano Artioli with Giampaolo Benedini. Above, two engineers checking an EB 110 prototype.

In the photo alongside, the designers from Modena, Tiziano Benedetti, Achille Bevini and Oliviero Pedrazzi constitute the historic nucleus of the Bugatti team. Brought into the EB 110 project by Romano Artioli, they began work on the design of the car even before the Campogalliano complex was built.

gan their careers at Lamborghini designing the most famous Gran Turismos produced at Sant'Agata Bolognese. Subsequently the "Three Musketeers" set up Tecnostile, a qualified external design team working on behalf of third parties. Romano Artioli managed to get them involved even before Campogalliano was built by transmitting to them his passion for the renaissance of the Bugatti marque.

Benedetti, Bevini and Pedrazzi decided to give up their well established business in order to dedicate themselves full time to the new EB 110 project. "Today — according to the three Modenese engineers — designers can make use of highly sophisticated instruments which help in the development of the project or by speeding up the process. In any case inspiration and creativity remain the determinant factors." Achille Bevini and Oliviero Pedrazzi are involved in the design and development of Bugatti's cars. Tiziano Benedetti, on the other hand, has been entrusted with the important sector of design for third parties. The engineer Pavel Rajmis, of Czechoslovakian origin, is the head

of the Bugatti experimental department. He studied at the Tatra technical high school and then graduated in Germany.

After a period with Hoffman, a company specialized in the production of test benches, he worked from 1978 to 1989 in the Audi research department, involved in various projects such as the development of four-wheel drive cars which, winning three World Rally Championships, made a considerable contribution to the relaunching of the Ingolstadt company. "Looking at the EB 110 — affirms Rajmis — you can immediately perceive the continuity of the Bugatti tradition.

A link which is found above all when you're at the wheel of this extraordinary Gran Turismo, so different from all the rest. It's an extreme car, capable of stratospheric performance, but at the same time it's docile, safe and easy to drive." The EB 110 has proved itself to be an extremely reliable car.

In the photo on the right, a shot of the production under the control of Stefano Mion. In the photo at the bottom of the facing page, Pavel Rajmis, head of the Experimental Department, with the Chief Test Driver Jean Philippe Vittecoq.

Particular attention has been dedicated to the study and production of the electrical and electronic system. The head of this sector, Fernando Gabellini, a man of great experience, came from Ferrari where he had worked for 22 years on the electrical vicissitudes of Maranello's competition and road cars. "The search for reliability — confirms Gabellini — requires constant verification and experimentation with new materials and features. It's a task that never finishes". One of the thorniest problems which the car manufacturers have to tackle concerns the complex type approval testing of its cars.

Within the Bugatti technical team it is *ingenere* Federico Trombi who is responsible for seeing that the product conforms to the current norms.

ƎB

He performed the same role for 11 years at Ferrari. "Today the relative norms — underlines Trombi — are not uniform and therefore it's impossible to construct a single car which meets all the legal requirements at the same time. As a consequence you have to undertake a diversified production in relation to the various markets". The production director, Stefano Mion, is the youngest member of the team. Graduating from Bologna in engineering with a technological-administrative bias, he worked for the helicopter manufacturer Agusta and for Lamborghini before arriving at Campogalliano in February, 1991.

Here he also has responsibility for buying, quality and maintenance. Very sophisticated instruments and craft-based tools coexist on the Bugatti production lines. "These two aspects which at first sight might seem antithetical — claims Mion — are in fact complementary. On the one hand technology supplies exceptional tooling which allow notable savings to be made in time as well as greater precision; on the other hand, craftsmanship, apart form being indispensable in very low volume production like ours, allows an individual to make a personal contribution to the finished product".

However, these individual talents are not enough. The whole structure composed of teams of the highest quality, specialized engineers for this firm which produces the fastest and highest performing Gran Turismo in the world, all the administrative staff, those involved in the constant servicing of an evolving factory, the Bugatti girls (90% of whom are graduates and English, French, German and Portuguese mother-tongue speakers) are the vital complement to the great "Bugatti orchestra" composed of 190 elements. When the orchestra plays the pieces, everybody has to pull their weight: it is this that makes the difference between being great and simply being an orchestra, and this is why there is no place at Bugatti for those who do not give their all in terms of concentration and team and professional spirit. It is from these things that the uniqueness of Bugatti is apparent. □

The car
on the track

FASTER THAN
THE WIND

*During the type approval testing carried out on the annular
Nardò track in Puglia, the EB 110 established a new world speed
record for series-built Gran Turismos, reaching 342 km/h.
An exceptional result for Bugatti and its team.*

BY GIANCARLO MARIANI — PHOTOS BY UMBERTO GUIZZARDI

Silence reigned and a light breeze blew in from the sea. We were at Nardò, in the South of Italy where unique vehicle testing facilities are to be found. In the distance a noise began to make itself heard, progressively growing in intensity. It was not an Air Force Tornado but an exceptional automobile: the Bugatti EB 110. In a flash it drew up to the measured line and the instruments were about to record an exceptional time. Everybody held their breath and it seemed as though the car was about to take off.

The wait to hear the result was very brief. The electronic instruments had recorded a sensational time. The tension suddenly disappeared and a great joy spread though those present and a spontaneous applause was directed at the driver who was already far away on the horizon. With a speed of 342 km/h the Bugatti had captured the world record for a series-built Gran Turismo. It was a moment of collective satisfaction for the team which had worked so hard to reach this objective. The Nardò mission was the culminating phase in the Type approval or homologation process which consists of the definition of the car's perfor-

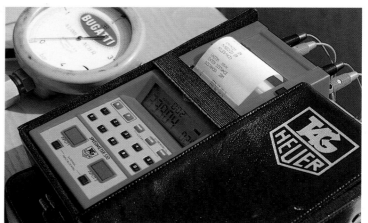

mance on the road. For this particular test the ring built in the province of Lecce in 1975 was chosen as, with a length of 12.6 km, it allows extremely high speeds to be reached in conditions of absolute safety. Prior to this event two sessions had been held which served to test the car and verify the reliability of a team composed of people coming from different backgrounds. During the first session three prototypes were used: the C7 and the C8 (C stands for the chassis in Carbonfibre) and the A5 (A stands for the Aluminium chassis). In the course of this track reconnaissance a number of problems of an organizational nature emerged. The optimum point for measuring the speed in both directions had to be established, given that the positive slopes in one direction become negative in the other and vice-versa. It was also necessary to take account of the wind. The C7 was the chosen car whilst the C8 was used as a mule. Fifteen days later we returned to the track for a further session of tests and more fine tuning of the cars so as to be as well prepared as possible.

Modifications were made to the rear suspension, to the stance and to the rear wing. Changes which made the car extremely safe at sustained high speeds. In order to gather the data relating to the speed of the car, Bugatti opted to use a system designed in-house which excluded the photoelectric cells, which can be disturbed by solar light, and the radar. Instead the system used bands of aluminium placed at a certain distance from one another. As the car passes the first band it triggers a timer, and passing the second band it transmits another impulse. Knowing the distance between the bands and the time elapsed between the two impulses, the speed of the car can be calcu-

→

lated. It is an extremely precise instrument. Here we were on the long-awaited 24th of May, the day programmed for the homologation. In the preceding tests no problems with the engine had been noted and the technical staff were fairly relaxed. Prior to reaching the measured zone the car had covered a springboard stretch of 5 kilometres. After having established the prestigious record of 342 km/h further runs followed to a total of three in one direction and three in the other. The differences in the speeds recorded were truly minimal, in the order of half a kilometre per hour. The result achieved is of great significance from a technical point of view as it was obtained on a track of constant curvature with an inclination which at that speed was not able to fully compensate for the centrifugal force value. Later in the day tests of acceleration from a standing start were carried out. It should be noted that the car weighed 1850

Below, An evocative image of the car on the banked track of the circuit in Puglia. The Nardò ring, 12.6 km long, was specifically designed for the car maufacturers' high speed testing.

Acceleration figures

From 0 to 100 km/h	3,46 s		
From 0 to 400 m.	11,4 s	Exit speed	200,4 km/h
From 0 to 1000 m.	20,7 s	Exit speed	259,7 km/h

Max speed

	Homologated speed	342 km/h

kg as it was ballasted to represent a full load with a passenger and baggage.

The results of these tests were also very significant with performance decidedly superior to that of the competition. The time taken to reach 100 km/h from a standing start was 3.46 seconds, 400 metres were covered in 11.4 seconds and the kilometre line was crossed in 20.7 seconds. An exceptional feature of these tests was the absence of wheelspin. The vehicle always kept in line as the torque was perfectly balanced between the front and rear axles.

In the third phase the tests for the homologation of the brakes took place and the official from the ministry was not satisfied with seeing the recordings of the stopping distances, but wanted to examine the car close-up. The norms require the car to brake to a halt from a speed 80% of the car's maximum. In this case that meant braking from 280 km/h. The technical vice-chairman of Bugatti Automobili, ingegnere Luciano Caruso also wished to witness the performance of the EB 110. An agreement was reached whereby the test driver was to remain on the central section of the track, whilst the other car carrying the two

ministry officials was to remain on the upper section travelling at around 200/220 kmH.

The Bugatti caught up, overtook on the inside and braked without any problems whatsoever, demonstrating incredible stability. The last braking tests were then carried out. A round of applause for the brilliant results obtained is certainly due to all the members of the Bugatti équipe present at Nardò. An équipe that performed as if it were a superorganized Formula One outfit. Congratulations to Stefano Bruni (mechanic), ingegnere Luciano Caruso (technical vice-chairman), Antonio Cavalli (homologation office), Fernando Gabellini (responsible for the electronic side of the whole car), Claudio Galletti (responsible for the engine electronics), Luca Giacomoni (homologation office), Daniele Golinelli (engineer), Alberto Manzini (electrician), ingegnere Nicola Materazzi (technical director), Giuseppe Montorsi (test driver), Pavel Rajmis (director of the experimental department), Gianpaolo Simonini (head of the chassis department), Andrea Stenico (Coachwork), Federico Trombi (head of the homologation department), Jean Philippe Vittecoq (chief test driver). □

A ROAD-BURNING SUPERSTAR

Bugatti's chief tester reveals the emotions felt when driving the world's fastest Gran Turismo. A car of extraordinary performance; stable, safe and easily driven.

BY JEAN PHILIPPE VITTECOQ — PHOTOS BY SANDRO BACCHI

DRIVING IMPRESSIONS

...When I heard Pavel's voice in the headset shouting "VERY GOOD, Philippe!", I knew that we'd succeeded in testing an exceptional car, one capable of travelling at over 340 km/h in complete safety..."

For the whole team present at Nardò, for Jean Marc Borel at the trackside and of course for me, it was a moment of intense joy and great relief.

We'd never been in doubt of course, but the homologation officials' timings are the only ones that count. We'd won our wager, we were the best.

On more than one occasion, before the achievement of this performance, I had had the opportunity of appreciating just how pleasant and efficient the EB 110 was to drive. The brief that Romano Artioli had presented to me was already impressive: "To be the best in terms of the car's performance and efficiency, with a few goodies to 'give you a hand', namely 12 cylinders, 4 turbos, 60 valves, 560 horses, a torque output of 60 m/kg and 4 driven wheels..." Thanks a lot Mr President... let's get to work!

A year and a half after I had received this crystal clear message, what pleasure and what pride driving the EB 110 aroused — even for an old testing hand like me!

This car gives an enormous sensation of power but, however, at the same time its character and handling are extremely docile; this was our first objective, We wanted the owner of this car to be able to drive it "almost" as if he were an experienced test driver himself, in all circumstances — in town at 50 km/h, on the track at 300 km/h, on dry surfaces or in the wet.

In order to obtain this result we carried out innumerable tests, but never with any element of danger. The technical decisions made by the Bugatti engineers were very useful to me as, right from the very first few metres in the mule, at the end of 1990, I felt that the car had been born under a good sign. The true development work began early in 1991 at Monza with the prototype A 2 (chassis in aluminium). I had to find out immediately if the EB 110 would respond to adjustments.

After a few (already quick) laps of the famous Italian track, I was reassured; the prototype reacted to even minimal modifications to the suspension geometry. The worse thing that can happen to a tester is to find himself saddled with a passive vehicle. The EB 110 responded well to my probing, thus giv-

continues on page 34

In spite of the EB 110 S's immense power it is safe and docile. Thanks to its sporting set-up, compact dimensions and light weight, it is at its best on fast, snaking roads.

DRIVING IMPRESSIONS

continues from page 30

ing me the necessary information. I felt things were going well.

In 1991 I worked with the four prototypes with aluminium chassis and the most important phase was the identification of a damping system capable of providing the right compromise between roadholding and comfort. The chassis had to absorb the stresses provoked by high speeds and also provide adequate comfort in town.

Numerous sprung dampers were tried, in all conditions. The results were positive but... At the same time, thanks to the four prototypes and my friend Loris Bicocchi we carried out testing on the engine, gearbox and drive train, and on the brakes because the biggest problem with a very powerful car lies not in getting it going very quickly, but rather in getting it to stop. We tested the brakes at the small airport at Carpi.

The testing rhythm was accelerated and in June, 1991 we went to the great Nürburgring circuit (the toughest test of a car's handling) to check out the EB 110's progress. In spite of certain teething troubles I was satisfied with its healthy and efficient behaviour with a lap (21 km and 176

The two Bugatti Gran Turismos, the EB 110 and the EB 110 S, portrayed together during testing on a tortuous route. Four-wheel drive provides the car with excellent roadholding in all conditions.

corners) being covered in 8' 15'. However, there was still much to be done and, above all, I could not wait to receive the carbonfibre chassis and the definitive bodywork. I got my hands on them after the official presentation at Paris where the parade along the Champs Elyseé left me with an indelible memory.

At the end of 1991 I received the definitive car for testing, the C7 (the C standing for Carbonfibre). To be sure I was expecting to find some difference compared with the aluminium chassis but I was stunned by the rigidity of the carbonfibre. The car's reactions were all more intense, more pre-

→

cise, to such an extent that I had to increase the vertical spring rates which were subjected to great stress by the chassis.

A slight modification to the frontal aerodynamics allowed us to obtain a very reassuring set-up at high speeds. Throughout the testing period, and every time it proved necessary, we went to check out the most

interesting solutions on the track. Thus I drove the EB 110 at Varano, Magione, Monza, Nardò, Nürburgring, Val di Vienne, Clermont Ferrand and Imola.

The open road, however, remains the best test bench of all.

The more sporting version fo the EB 110, lighter and more powerful, has been designed for those who look for performance

→

Diavia

The EB 110 was *born out of a technological synergy running between French and Italian industries, utilizing avant-garde features in all areas: from the coachwork to the power-train to individual components. Thus it could hardly fail to require a component of fundamental importance to comfort and safety: the air conditioner, production of which has been entrusted to the experts at Diavia. Parallel to the development of the overall project, after two and a half years of research and testing in controlled climate conditions, Diavia has produced a made-to-measure climate control system which synthesizes the most advanced and functional features which current thermodynamic technology is able to offer. We asked Giancarlo Mantellini, Managing Director of Diavia, how his company had gone about creating a product for Bugatti.*

"Diavia made recourse to an ample condenser placed in front of the car's water radiator. The heart of the system comprises two heat exchangers: one air-to-freon and the other air-to-water. The compressor is linked to an automatic cut-off system: an important automatic safety device.

The Diavia air conditioner is incredibly efficient: the data recorded in the controlled-climate lab demonstrate that it betters the United States norms, the strictest in the world. It is an exceptional performance which is also obtained in the most extreme of operating conditions with a sophisticated and ultra-light system: its overall weight is just 18 kg!"

The system is extremely easy to use thanks to the clarity of the luminous display and the excellent ergonomics of the controls: it is a fully automatic system (with, however, the possibility of manual operation), controlled by a computer which elaborates the data emitted by the sensors and acts to maintain the desired temperature imposed by the occupants of the car.

The Diavia air conditioning system for the Bugatti EB 110 is also equipped with the "Purimax" device which prevents polluted air from entering the cabin, filtering the pollutants and activating the recirculation system. The Bugatti EB 110's

climate control system coalesces perfectly with the futuristic conception that inspired the production of this high class Gran Turismo; it is sophisticated and reliable and represents the highest expression of avant-garde thermodynamics... and carries the Diavia name.

The working principle behind the air conditioning system is based on the capacity of the refrigerating fluid to absorb or release heat in significant quantities when it undergoes changes in its physical state: from liquid to gas and vice versa.

The compressor, driven off the crankshaft via a belt and an electromagnetic coupling, takes in the refrigerant in its gaseous state at low pressure and low temperature, and compresses it to the point where its temperature is higher than that of the outside air. The refrigerant expelled from the compressor enters the condenser at this temperature and under high pressure.

Within the compressor it undergoes a transformation of its physical state: from the gaseous state it turns into a liquid, shedding heat to the external air which crosses it through the dynamic effect caused by the vehicle's movement, or generated artificially by one or more of the electric fans in the engine compartment.

The liquid refrigerant emerging from the condenser passes through the dehydration filter which removes the humidity as well as any solid impurities and directs it towards the expansion valve.

Passing through the expansion valve the refrigerant undergoes a drastic reduction in pressure to values which correspond to a temperature lower than that in the cabin. From the expansion valve, the refrigerant enters directly into the evaporator and, passing through, again changes state: from liquid to gas, absorbing in the process the heat from the air taken from the cabin, ducted through the evapo-

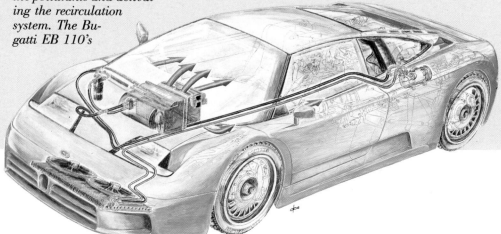

In the photo on this page, the two cars tackling a fast S-bend in the mountains.

rator and readmitted into the cabin cool and dehumidified. The change in the physical state of the refrigerant is due to the effect of the heat extracted from the air present in the cabin which, flowing over the cool surface of the evaporator, is itself cooled in turn and directed back into the cabin via a fan, thus lowering the cabin temperature.

The treated air emitted into the cabin is also dehumidified as the water vapour content is in part condensed as it comes into contact with the cold parts of the evaporator; the liquid which thus collects is drained away through one or more waste tubes. Coming out of the evaporator, the refrigerant in its gaseous state and at low pressure is taken in by the compressor again and the cycle starts over.

The performance of the system is controlled through a thermostat and a commutator which regulate the temperature of the refrigerant and the speed of the ventilation system of the evaporator itself.

A safety pressure switch disengages the compressor's electromagnetic coupling when pressure is either too high or too low and activates the electric fan again in relation to the pressure existing in the circuit. □

DRIVING IMPRESSIONS

above all else from their Gran Turismos. The driving position is more sporting than that of the standard EB 110. The racing seats and the twin shoulder harnesses guarantee improved lateral support for the body. The EB 110 S is less docile to drive and more responsive than its sister car with even greater braking and acceleration qualities.

The special tyres developed by Michelin make a decisive contribution to the new Bugatti's roadholding.

The Campogalliano engineers spent a considerable amount of time working in collaboration with their opposite numbers from Clermont Ferrand to adapt the structure, the

compound and the dimensions of the ultra-low profile MXX3 radials to the chassis and the sophisticated suspension system of the EB 110. Initially 17' tyres were mounted but these were later replaced by 18' covers. In this way the EB 110 has been able to benefit from the latest developments introduced by Michelin in the field of ultra-high performance tyres.

The definitive dimensions both for the EB 110 and the S are: 245/40 ZR 18 at the front, and 325/30 ZR 18 at the rear. Given an equivalent rolling circumference with the 18' rim diameter, the tyre sidewall is

Above, the Bugattis accelerating out of a curve. On the facing page a front view of the EB 110 in action on a hump.

lower and therefore roadholding is improved and tyre drift is reduced. At the same time by using a larger diameter wheel the Bugatti engineers have been able to fit larger diameter brakes and improve brake cooling. In spite of the fact that the Michelin MXX3 tyres destined for the EB 110 are designed to cope with extremely high performance they create very little rolling noise, provid-

the testers this is always a moment of mixed emotions, of joy and sadness. Joy at presenting their creations to the world, and sadness at the thought of separation. However, there will be other Bugattis which, I am sure, will again provide me with great satisfaction.

When testing a car the driver is never alone. At his shoulder stands an entire com-

ing excellent, vibration-free acoustic comfort. Another positive feature is that they have always lasted for over 15,000 km in all the testing we carried out. The development of the EB 110 is currently still underway because there is always much to be done to remain on top, and the testing of a model does not come to an end when it goes into production.

The fortunate owners will soon be taking delivery of their technological 'jewel'. For

pany, especially its Experimental team.

And now that the EB 110 has gone out into the world I would like to thank my mechanic friends who performed miracles to make sure that the car was always ready on time for the test sessions. When it was necessary they worked themselves to the bone, day and night. Therefore, to Loris, Stefano, Roby, Robertone, Moli, Claudio, Massimo, Dotta... and all the others: MANY THANKS! ☐

Technical
Dossier

COMPRESSORS AND TURBOS: TWO GENERATIONS HEAD TO HEAD

In 1926 Ettore Bugatti was converted to supercharging, introducing a volumetric compressor on the Type 35 in order to keep on winning. Today the EB 110 is equipped with four turbos from the word go.

BY ENRICO BENZING

The EB 110 challenges the Type 35B to a sprint.
On the the right a view of the Type 35B's supercharger.

Supercharging links — but also divides — the mechanical layout of the EB 110 of the Bugatti renaissance and that of a considerable part of the sporting production of the great Ettore Bugatti himself. The differences are quite understandable: almost seventy years of technological development separate the devices under consideration.

On the one hand is the volumetric compressor directly driven off the crankshaft, and therefore responsible for the absorption of a considerable amount of power; on the other is the turbo which uses the enthalpic energy of the exhaust gases (that is, an energy of pressure and heat which is normally →

On the left-hand page, top, the Type 35B charging at full speed along the Campogalliano track. Below, the new EB 110 flanks her forebear underneath the company badge. In the small photo on the right, the two cars in action.

dispersed) with negligible power absorption levels (from exhaust back pressure).

On one point, however, the automotive genius of the Twenties and Thirties and the engineering school recently established at Campogalliano are in perfect accord: their conception of the use of the supercharger.

EB

Not as a means of immoderately increasing peak power output, at the expense of usability, but rather as an efficient system of rounding out the functionality of the engine, with all efforts concentrated on the improvement of thermodynamic efficiency (now also important for minimum atmospheric pollution) and volumetric efficiency. In a word, progress, through advanced research. In fact a car of the status of the EB 110, as sporting as it is luxurious, has to take its place at the summit of current technological development in the most elegant of manners; that is to say with the greatest degree of driveability possible. We should say right away that today's engineers have an advantage: they can apply forced induction with guarantees of reliability and functionality unthinkable once upon a time (a supercharged Royale would have been unfeasible). This is due to developments in metallurgy, petrochemistry and, above all, to the electronic revolution, an extraordinarily potent resource for the control of fuel supply, ignition and all the parameters regarding the turbocharger.

Ettore Bugatti — it is as well to remember — came to supercharging rather late (1926), and allowed himself to be converted for purely competition reasons. It was an absolute necessity in the field of Grand Prix cars where the first supercharger had been introduced back in 1923, on the Fiat "805" in the French G.P. at Tours, and where it had rapidly become a common feature. Initially Bugatti had been reluctant to use superchargers for various technical reasons,

but also on ethical grounds: in 1923 the French constructors had harshly accused Fiat of infractions of the regulations and intended to take legal action as supercharging completely overturned the engine technology of the time. The regulations, which only went as far as limiting total cylinder capacity to a maximum of 2,000 c.c., referred

to engines currently in use, and not to radically different features.

In 1924, a Bugatti Type 35 with a normally aspirated, in-line, 8-cylinder (60x88 mm) engine displacing 1,991 c.c. produced 90 hp at 6,000 rpm; the previous year the supercharged 8-cylinder 405 developing 120 hp fitted to the Fiat 805 had already achieved the following increases compared with the normally aspirated engine: 32% in maximum power and 13.5% in mean effective pressure, quantity proportional to the torque. Again in 1924, at the start of the French Grand Prix at Lyon, four marques out of seven (Fiat, Alfa Romeo — victorious with the memorable P2 — Miller and

→

Sunbeam) used supercharged 2-litre engines; then came Talbot and, in 1925, Delage with nothing less than a blown 12-cylinder unit.

Thus, after the early controversy, supercharging became virtually obligatory. Bugatti joined the club with his usual style: he called the top specialist of the time, Edmondo

The first Bugatti supercharger was of the type with twin, three-lobed rotors (machined from solid metal), mounted on ball bearings in a 185 mm³-long stator. It was a device notable for its extreme simplicity and the quality of its execution: at that time tolerances of one hundredth of a millimetre were not easily obtained. It rotated at the same speed

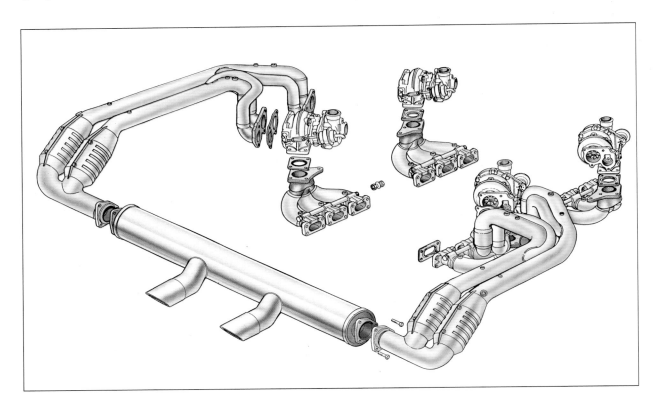

Moglia, fresh from the Talbot projects, to Molsheim. As early as August, 1925 he was in possession of the first drawings of a refined supercharger.

He then exploited the innovation in the most profitable of manners and used it, for engines in the 2,000 — 2,300 c.c. category (known as the Type 35 B or 35 TC and 35 C) in the development of other cars such as those meeting the regulations for the Targa Florio (five consecutive victories) or those of Formula Libre.

as the engine and produced relative boost pressures in the order of 0.35 — 0.45 bar. In a single bound maximum power output was increased from 120 to 135 hp. A significant detail should be recorded: the debut victory in the Alsace Grand Prix at Strasbourg in May, 1926 (the winner was André Dubonnet and there were also Count Aymo Maggi and Pierre De Vizcaya) was obtained by a Type 35 with an engine capacity reduced to 1,100 c.c., red-lined at 6,300 rpm rather than 6,000. It was in this year that the Grand Prix formula engine capacity was reduced from 2,000 to 1,500 c.c. (in order to reduce power outputs) and this experiment was to

Above, the turbocharging layout adopted on the EB 110. Right, top, in the foreground, the Type 35B's supercharger. Below, a detail of the turbo fitted to the EB 110.

→

prove providential: after all 1926 was to be Bugatti's year.

From the past we move into the present; the supercharging theme is still at the heart of avant-garde engine technology: we are already aware of the major design features of the V12 engine fitted to the EB 110; what still remains to be discovered regards its functionality. The primary objective of delivering 550-600 hp (normal and "S" versions) in a modern supercar with a limited total displacement (reducing weight and bulk), according to a ratio a little over 1.4:1 (5,000 c.c. normally aspirated, 3.500 c.c. supercharged), would be relatively easy for all in the light of current turbo technology. And then? The quadratic law applying to the turbine gives virtually zero boost pressure at minimum revs, only to proceed with a spectacular thrust towards the peak power speed. At 2,000 revs, a 3,500 cm³ turbo engine with a compression ratio of 7.5:1 would be comparable to a poor normally aspirated engine of equal capacity; only when it reached 8,500 would it give anything away to an "atmospheric" five-litre.

New technologies which maintain the superiority of the engine's efficiency are now available, and merit careful study.

Most importantly, Bugatti's power unit engineers have opted for a parallel multi-turbo set-up which releases the supercharging effect from its dependency on the size of the turbine (large dimensions favour maximum power, small dimensions favouring efficiency at low revs). Four IHI turbines of the most advanced type are fitted (52 & 54 mm in diameter for the normal engine and the sporting version), specifically assembled for this application and featuring efficient water cooling.

The system is completed by the inevitable air-to-air intercooler. Thus all the most unimaginable trickery has a part to play: the boost pressure curve has been designed in such a way as to reach its peak (1.05 — 1.10 bar of relative pressure) at around 3,800 rpm (4,000 rpm in the "S" version) where

Borgo-Nova

Borgo-Nova, *a company specializing in components for high-tech cars and part of the international T&N group, has developed in collaboration with Bugatti the "cylinder assembly" for the engine of the new EB 110, using innovative solutions in terms of design and materials.*

The Bugatti engine's cylinder assembly is undoubtedly the area subjected to greatest stress in the entire car. It has had to be been designed to withstand the enormous loadings of pressure and temperature characteristic of this high *performance unit delivering no less than 160 hp per litre in the Supersport version. Furthermore, it has to be capable of operating in ambient temperatures ranging from -40° to +50°. It must be as quiet as possible to pass the extremely severe type approval testing and also be free of the famous "blow-by" problem — the leakage of oil into the combustion chamber preventing the car from passing the toxic exhaust emissions tests, and the leakage of combustion gases into the crankcase leading to the loss of lubricant.*

Furthermore, the assembly has to be reliable over *thousands of kilometres which, in the case of the Bugatti, are sure to be hard-driven kilometres.*

The principal characteristics are as follows:
* "X piston" lightweight piston (see photo) This product, designed and patented by Borgo-Nova, provides advantages in terms of:
- a reduction in the reciprocating masses and vibration,
- reduced friction,
- reduced noise
- improved performance (consumption and power).
* Piston rings of extremely reduced axial thickness fol- *lowing the most up-to-date engineering trends.*
* Aluminium cylinder liners with bearing surfaces treated with the SILBORN process guaranteeing the lightness and resistance to wear required by the high performance of the Bugatti engines.

The collaboration between Bugatti and Borgo-Nova has led to the development of components of which both companies are very proud, but this is only the beginning as further versions are being developed and new engines will be able to take advantage of these exceptional components. □

the maximum torque of 620 Nm or 63.2 kgm (637 Nm or 65 kgm for the "S") is delivered; from here on up to the peak power speed, boost pressure progressively decreases, down to a value of around 0.75 bar.

The pressure release valve or wastegate is controlled by electrovalves and is electronically managed by the same ECU that integrates all of the fuel supply and ignition operations (as well as piloting the Lambda probe for the catalyser) through complex mapping. The information parameters are the usual rpm, throttle opening angle, boost pressure and air and water temperature figures.

It is no longer necessary to talk about delay in the turbo response. The unusual disposition of the units, one per group of three cylinders, has meant however that considerable problems have had to be resolved regarding synchronization and the fluid mechanics of the manifolds (variations in the density of the flow), in order to guarantee maximum homogeneity in the distribution of the compressed air. What should be talked about on the other hand are the notable technical conquests: a specific consumption of just 200 gr/Hp-hour at peak torque speed, with reductions of 10-20 gr/Hp-hour compared with the

best normally aspirated engines. High efficiency required a five-valve per cylinder timing system — the ideal solution with turbo-charged engines, which can compensate for the losses in the manifolds — and capacitive discharge ignition.

Developments in the future might well include differentiated opening of the three intake valves and variations in ignition advance cylinder per cylinder, as used in Formula 1 engines. Two knock sensors, one per group of six cylinders, complete the range of information supplied to the extensive electronic engine management system, after the experimental phase, on the super-fast Nardò circuit with average speeds of 342 km/h, had seen the use of over 40 sensors and thermocouples for a wide-ranging data input.

In this way the Bugatti V12, using normal 95 NO lead-free petrol, boasts an unmatched functionality, from the quiet smoothness of delivery at low revs to the fullness of the mid-ranges on up to the rocket-like thrust at maximum power.

It all contributes to the driveability of a car which — all things being equal — can be taken well beyond the dictates and the spirit of Ettore Bugatti. □

TEAM-WORK

A broad stroke of blue lent colour to the tenth edition of the Mille Miglia retrospective. Eleven teams started, eleven finished. There was success beyond all expectations for the Équipe Bugatti.

BY DANIELA KETTMEIR

Rothlauf, Ernsting, Van Esser, Steele, Oprey, Lewis, Heimann, Reck, Manara, Guasti and others took part with their Bugattis. They were the oldest exhibits in the Mille Miglia's "travelling museum". And they finished ahead of the competitors in their category. They were all 50-60 years old. Eleven of them left Brescia... and they all finished!!

Bugatti Automobili offered technical assistance to this new team.

The idea stemmed from Fausto Manara, an enthusiast who then brought honour to the team by finishing 2nd in class and in the top 20 overall, along with Gianni Torel-

→

1000 MIGLIA →

In the large photo, preliminary scrutineering in Piazza della Vittoria, Brescia. Centre, the inaugural toast before the start. Below, the Bugatti Type 49 of Oprey-Van Hees at the start. Alongside, Bugattis at scrutineering.

1000 MIGLIA →

Large photo, the Type 35B of Guasti-Bazzi, 4th, 1st Class A. Small photos, left, from top to bottom, the Type 44 of Heymann-Soland, the Bugatti van and an emergency operation by mechanic Torelli. In the small photo on the facing page, the Kleine-Schutz team on the Raticosa pass.

li, restorer, and Ivo Ceci, the curator of the Centro Culturale Bugatti.

Renata and Romano Artioli set the preparations for the expedition in motion.

We left with two cars equipped with all that a "Bugattista" might dream of needing. We loaded the vehicles with cans of oil of different densities, made-to-measure for the various types of cars, equipment and tools, Ettore Bugatti "Cuvée Speciale Millesimée" champagne and lastly the team uniforms of blue jackets and caps.

The marque groups soon gathered in the square at Brescia and we of the Ettore Bugatti team lined up our 11 competitors among the 315 participants. We left under

→

1000
MIGLIA >

The revival of the classic Italian road race offers competitors the chance to experience the nation's historic and artistic patrimony. This page, the Bugattis in Piazza del Campo, Siena and at the Arena in Verona. Facing page, top left, the historic centre of Gubbio. Bottom and right, the Cathedral at Orvieto.

driving rain which we were to encounter again at San Marino. At Ferrara we slept on the boxes and cans for perhaps 4 hours after having the cars entrusted to Torelli oiled and watered. We met up with our German champion, Jürgen Ernsting in the square at Urbino. He restarted with help from Torelli. Ernsting never gave up and thus was to become one of the three prize winners from the "Équipe Bugatti". Torelli succeeded in reconstructing a magneto in just half an hour by using improvised parts taken from various cars of uncertain pedigree. Then came, for the first time in the history of this event, the route over the Terminillo through a hailstorm of biblical proportions from which

→

1000 MIGLIA ➤

This year bad weather again characterized the race. On the facing page, landscapes in the rain. Above, in the large photo, the Type 35A of Reck-Wurth in the sudden snow storm on the Terminillo. In the small photo, right, the arrival of the Type 37A of Rothlauf-Klaus.

emerged Guasti and Manara in 12th and 14th places. The Equipe's mechanics worked flat out at Rome, most of the cars needing attention. We slept for 2-3 hours but some spent all night with the cars.

The most Italian part of the event were the spectators who displayed an incredible warmth and interest. Each time we passed through a village we were given an emotional welcome.

At the end of the event our happy and faithful band felt as though they had been pampered, tended, backed up and protected by the technical assistance from the Équipe, and they had dared, with great faith and courage to complete the Mille Miglia inspired by the Guasti-Bazzi victory. □

CLOSE, BLUE ENCOUNTERS

For two days the Emilian Apennines were the stage for a historic revival. Eight Molsheim masterpieces gathered at Campogalliano for a regularity run quite unlike any other.

BY IVO CECI

The rev counter's hovering between 3500 and 4000 with the engine underlining the fact with an acute, exciting roar. Optimum revs maintained with continuous, rapid movements of the gear lever, each curve is tackled with the steering wheel firmly grasped and the *bolide* tenaciously gripping the asphalt and cornering as if on two invisible rails. What can beat a tortuous road through the Apennines on a sunny day in a thundering Type 43?

There's no doubt that the "Grand Sport" is still capable of setting pulses racing and, even though we're used to the hyper-performance of today's supercars, its dazzling acceleration still arouses surprise and admiration. It's not surprising really as back in distant 1927, when it was first introduced, it could proudly boast the title of the world's fastest touring car and, was quite capable of taking a few Sunday races in its stride.

After hundreds of curves and a few hours of enjoyable driving here we are at our destination on a hot Saturday afternoon at the end of May. The other Bugattis join us immediately, rumbustiously filling the car- →

The photos show episodes in the first Rally dei Castelli Matildici organized by the Italian Bugatti Club. The participants especially enjoyed themselves on the loose surfaces and on the tortuous roads of the Apennines. There was also a classic motorcycle as a courier.

The Bugatti
Rally, won by
Fausto Manara
in a Type 40A
cabriolet, was
rich in historic
and panoramic
sights which
thrilled all the
competitors.
Some of them
demonstrated
truly prodigious
driving.

park, rupturing the ancient tranquillity of the place and filling the air with the scent of speed and power as they finally come to rest at the foot of the Castello di Matilde. Centuries-old ruins look loftily down and there's still something in the air of the solem-

Top, the passing of two Bugattis through the rich green landscape of the Modena region. To the right, the rally prizegiving. In the course of the gala evening there were also celebrations for the teams which took part in the 1000 Miglia.

nity of the events of almost a thousand years ago: the defeat and humiliation of an emperor, Henry IV. This is the setting for the first stopover of the "1st Rally Castelli Matildici" organized by the Bugatti Club Italia to celebrate its renaissance and to bring together a group of friends around a common idea: the love of Bugatti motor cars. There are also a number of foreign guests, survivors of the Mille Miglia, and they're also enjoying themselves on those roads, im-

mersed in one of the most beautiful panoramas in the Italian Apennines, which make driving their Grand Prix machines such a pleasure.

The start of the Rally had taken place in the morning within the grounds of the Campogalliano factory where, welcomed by Romano Artioli, the Bugatti enthusiasts raced, challenging each other with chronometers and broadslides. It was a truly competitive race with just 7 thousandths of a second separating the first- and second-placed cars. Fausto Manara with his Type 40 A gained his revenge over Francesco Guasti and his 35 C, thus reversing the result of the 1000 Miglia of the previous week and finally giving a tranquil touring machine the chance to put a rich grid of snorting Grand Prix models in their places.

The rally then proceeded for two days, with climbs, descents, curves, traffic-free roads and the odd stretch of loose surface all contributing to the participant's entertainment.

The landscape, the places visited and, why not, the tasty local cuisine made an enormous contribution to the success of the Italian Bugattiphiles' first outing which ended in the castle belonging to the hospitable Mario Righini who, while being one of the best known Alfa Romeo collectors, is not immune to the Bugattis' appeal. In fact his splendid collection includes a unique vehicle which would be the pride and joy of any Bugatti enthusiast: a twin-engined Prinetti e Stucchi tricycle, a product of the precocious genius of Ettore Bugatti and admirably conserved for almost one hundred years. On this occasion it was displayed in the entrance court and as the Bugattis arrived they were lined up around it, almost as if they were paying homage to a noble forebear. Finally there was the visit to the Campogalliano factory which included certain Top Secret areas like the Experimental Department where we had a chance to admire the EB 110 S back from its 342 km/h world record speed run. It was a worthy conclusion to an event which, given the enthusiasm of those taking part, should become an annual not-to-be-missed event. □

A MAN, A MYTH AN ADVENTURE

Flashes of enamel, painted panels. Light blue cotton overalls, roads of white dust, silk flags blowing in the wind. Cars, races and drivers. The Thirties were years to grasp hurriedly, on the trail of a Futurist frenzy. There's no trace of colour in the photos or in the memory. And yet the colours were there, and in abundance. They were flags of war, symbols of an origin, of a difference. Italian red, French blue. Achille Varzi decided to make his debut at the wheel of a British racing green Bugatti. The year was 1926 and it was a deliberate gesture, a disassociation. The first of an infinite series.

Chapter two also had an air of wayward independence and rebellion. The year:
→

Achille Varzi: confident, cool and calculated on the track. A winning style which found many followers. His image, washed in light blue, behind the Bugatti horseshoe radiator is part of racing history. His memorable duels with Nuvolari divided nations.

BY GIORGIO TERRUZZI

*Above, Achille Varzi at the wheel
of a Bugatti Type 35 C with his eternal rival
Tazio Nuvolari back in 1929. Below,
the Galliate-born driver in a Bugatti Type 59.*

1928. Tazio Nuvolari and Achille Varzi together in the same team. Again Bugattis, this time light blue. No more motorcycles: the two great warriors had decided to stay together for a while, to investigate a strange similarity. And in order to understand and to be understood they had no need of the Italian concensus, the approbation provided by that particular red. Five races were sufficient to establish a definite antagonism and to assign the roles. Varzi assumed the more uncomfortable, more in keeping with a shadowed character.

This was the perfect moment for the colour red to set the challenge alight, to split Italian opinion. Two years, 1929 and 1930 at the wheel of the Alfa Romeo. But Varzi was an uncontrollable driver, cold, even too sure of himself. A racing intellectual, a rich man. He offered the public an instinctive technical perfection. His immediately legendary style needed no forcing or gratifications. The straight parting of his hair, the impeccable crease in his trousers, the precise line through a corner all belonged to the same culture, to a fully coherent philosophy. He was liked, inevitably so; he

the battlefield, two coloured dots to follow with the naked eye, with binoculars or in the imagination. Nuvolari was the white knight, a figure that played unconsciously into the hands of Fascism. Varzi became an obstacle, a spiteful, persistent flash of blue. But he was also an accomplice, an indispensable element in a magnificent game, in an unrepeatable era.

The great spectacle was staged on the tracks and roads of Europe and the grand finale was held at Montecarlo on the 23rd of April, 1933. One hundred laps, a relentless chase. A two-way match which Varzi won by racing, just for once, and only for once, the way Nuvolari raced. Achille could not tolerate defeat and more than a year had passed since his last victory. Far too long for that very un-Italian gentleman, and for that so very French automobile. First overall at Montecarlo, first overall at Tripoli, first overall at Avus. The elegant forms of the Bugatti and the extremely elegant gestures of the gentleman from Galliate had taken, once again, centre stage. And everybody had to applaud.

That image of Varzi behind the oval Bugatti radiator has remained on the asphalt, on the beaten earth without losing even a fragment of its strength. It is a joyful image, charged with sky-blue, with liberty. It contains something intense that Achille never found as he moved towards the red of the Scuderia Ferrari or towards the silver of the Auto Union team: the electric, ferocious determination of a young man still capable of facing up to his own solitude. □

On the facing page, top, Achille Varzi in his famous light blue racing overalls. Below, in coversation with the designer Vittorio Jano. Above, again Varzi with Borzacchini victorious at Susa Moncenisio in 1931.

was a winner. Above all he liked himself. Everything else was of little importance. In order to continue racing on his own terms Varzi returned to Bugatti. Between the two names there was clearly an elective affinity, an anomalous courage and an extraordinary pride. But there was also an extremely high price to be paid every Sunday in the form of popularity. Varzi and Bugatti were running uphill, against the tide. They were Italian only in name, gone over to the other side, enemies. An adventure charged with anger, speed and noise. Three years to write a chapter of racing history, contributing to the legend of that pair of formidable drivers which had never appeared so divided, yet so harmonious. Two splashes of colour on

IN THE REALM OF FORMULA 1

In 1929, 1930, 1931 and 1933 the Bugattis triumphed in the Montecarlo Grand Prix. Sixty-three years after the first victory the EB 110 returned to the Prince's court as a protagonist.

BY GIANNI SIGHINOLFI

1992 saw Bugatti's return to Montecarlo with an invitation to present the new EB 110 to the royal family. The principality celebrated the fiftieth edition of its Formula 1 Grand Prix this year. The first edition in 1929 was dominated by the Type 35 B's of Williams and Bouriano. The Molsheim cars won again in 1930, 1931 and 1933. The victorious Bugatti in 1929 developed 140 hp giving a maximum speed of over 200 km/h. The current EB 110 offers four times as much power and a top speed of 342 km/h.

Sixty-three years separate this presentation and Bugatti's first victory in the Principality. The Monacans are well aware that their sovereign is a lover of fine cars. He possesses a collection of 90 vehicles, of which 66 are in perfect working order. His only regret is that he does not possess the jewel of his dreams: a Bugatti 57 S.

It was this Bugatti tradition which stirred the Prince's interest in its latest creations. The official presentation took place in the courtyard of the Grimaldi Palace, in the presence of Michel Bugatti, Jean Marc Borel, Chairman of Bugatti International Holding, Gian Paolo Benedini, Vice-chairman of Bugatti Automobili and Renata Kettmeir Artioli, Chairperson of Ettore Bugatti Srl. It was held on Friday, the 29th of May. The cars aroused enormous interest among those present, and also among the public. The Crown Prince was able to enjoy first-hand experience of their capabilities when he took the wheel for a few laps of the famous circuit. ☐

On these pages, the salient episodes of the Bugatti expedition to Montecarlo. The EB 110 S on the track, the cars waiting for the start, the official presentation in the courtyard of the Grimaldi Palace in the presence of Prince Ranieri, and Prince Albert behind the wheel of the car.

Jean Marc Borel, Chairman of Bugatti International, was the promoter of this unique Bugatti expedition to the court of Prince Ranieri.

A QUESTION OF IMAGE

*A group of specialists with the task of defending and promoting
the Bugatti Marque and style throughout the world are
at work at Ettore Bugatti, in a modern, functional complex at Ora.*

BY GIUSEPPE MAGHENZANI

Before crossing the threshold of what is a very special "factory" — Ettore Bugatti at Ora — it would be as well to sketch in a few details about its background. We are not talking about the fabulous backdrop provided by the Alps overlooking the town, or the trees and greenery which surround the buildings or the attractive water garden at the entrance. Rather we are talking about certain questions that are, as you might say, a little out of fashion and forgotten. As forgotten as they are important to the understanding of why the Bugatti name lives on here today, and just why it would be impossible for it to live elsewhere. Just clear your minds for a moment of all thoughts of day-to-day shopping, the designer labels in the

windows, the junk mail you find in your letterboxes, and try tuning into a different symphony in this material world, a world in which it seems to be all too easy to create instant, ephemeral legends. There exists in fact an aspect of design and product which is by no means on the borders of reality. It consists of seeking out and discovering the style and spirit of objects that are designed as such, that is to say beautiful, attractive and functional objects. That they are of a certain class is a consequence for those who admire them - as a possessor and certainly not as a consumer - for their authenticity. If the product is 'true' it is considerably more than a mere sign of distinction.

The epic Bugatti story, in its most intimate

experiences, belongs to this way of looking at things, where objects acquire value through the relationship they establish with those who use them and the innovation and design process which lie behind them. If indeed a "Bugatti Style" actually existed, there is a need today to propose, with all due respect for the times, the same kind of exclusiveness capable of transmitting to the world signals of class under the aegis of perfection and a never dormant cultural memory. What is the function of an object if it is not the consummation of a rite? What relationship is there between the imagination and the material, beyond any preconceived dogmas? A philosophy common to

→

In the photo above, the staff directed by Mrs Renata Kettmeir, Chairperson of Ettore Bugatti. On the facing page, above the title, the telephone switchboard; below, the spacious hall of the Centre designed by the architect Ambrosini.

In the photo on the left, the bust of Ettore Bugatti; right, work in progress in the firm's legal department.

all the Bugatti family has happily come full circle and we are thinking of products for our era that have a reserve of beauty and stylistic passion. With this thought it is as if we have already crossed the Ettore Bugatti threshold on an itinerary from the project to the factory, and from the product to its owner without the interruption of *emotions*.

Ettore's genius effectively had the capacity to transfer a creative vision into an immediate visible sign. This *intuitive* vision also lives on in the present, in the respect for the criteria which made it famous. The use of research for example, the defence of the company, and with the introduction of objects designed for the present day (neither replicas nor revivals) and with due respect for an exclusive Bugatti tradition: the tradition of *Perfection*. The EB-Ettore Bugatti marque is thus a clear and explicit reference to this theme. This is why Ettore's signature, stamped many years ago on the engine of the Type 13 Brescia has a permanent home at Ora. The factory that we are about to visit is therefore a marque which guarantees an entrepreneurial philosophy which is also a philosophy of life.

To protect this precious image, the Ettore Bugatti legal department defends the marque throughout the world (on behalf of both Ettore Bugatti and Bugatti Automobili). It

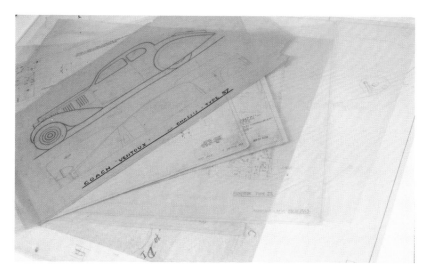

produces a good few hundredweight of paper a year, uses countless stamps, and is a world-wide eye witness. Being custodians of a marque, however, means being capable of protecting and conserving first, foremost, and as well as possible, an iconographic, technical and cultural patrimony of great value.

In the company's entrance hall there is a small, but very select museum: works of the Bugatti family are exhibited. There are

→

Above, original drawings owned by the Cultural Centre at Ora. On the facing page, top, Mrs Renata Kettmeir with secretary Mary Johnson; bottom, Bruno Telchini and Luigi Palladino of the legal department defending and promoting of the Bugatti marque.

Mrs Daniela Kettmeir is responsible for the archive and contacts with the Bugatti clubs around the world. In the photo top right, a panorama of the signatures of the engineers forming the Bugatti team at Molsheim in the first decades of this century. Right, a detail of the photographic display in the hall and, bottom, the writing desk made by Carlo Bugatti exhibited in the centre's museum.

pieces that have arrived here from all over the world and bear testimony to the cultural and artistic life of the family.

The Bugatti's formal adventure — father Carlo, creator of Art Nouveau furniture, brother Rembrandt, talented animal sculptor and son Jean, the designer of superb coachwork — took place at the end of the nineteenth century and during the first forty years of this century. It thus coincides with the most important period of another cultural adventure, that of the artistic avant-garde of the twentieth century.

Modernity and the twilight of Romanticism constitute the two poles of this adventure. On the other hand one could hardly speak the language of speed without these two reference points. There are certainly contradictions, those which lead Ettore to turn his melancholic gaze towards the past (one thinks of his love of horses and the "Fiacre" style). However, in our case we can consign to history a truly rare pair of opposites: an antique flavour and the modernity of innovation. Bugatti is the happy synthesis of these two aspects. In the rich archives where around 40,000 original drawings and documents are conserved, the cataloguing operation (which will last three years) keeps alive the firm's history. On the walls, as well as reproductions and original posters, innumerable signs stand out: they are the signatures of the Bugatti engineers,

In the photo above, at work in the conference room at the Bugatti Styling Centre.
In the photo to the left, Susanna Da Cortà, product head, alongside an exhibit.
In the photo here alongside, Silvia Frangipane at the drawing board during her working day.

the same that are found on the autograph technical drawings in the archives. Furthermore the company's entrance hall contains an interesting photographic record spanning more than a century: from the young Ettore to the presentation of the EB 110 in Paris. Archive, Museum, Cultural Centre... Out of the company's care for its own roots not only stem events, rallies, initiatives and contacts with all the Bugatti Clubs throughout the world, but the very design philosophy itself, and the ability to discern what will, and what will never be Bugatti also takes shape.

The Bugatti Styling Centre is the heart of the company. It is the generator of the idea and the reality of the products which are subsequently commercialized through international agreements drawn up with leading companies in the various fields. Ettore Bugatti's commercial policy also tends to designate the points of sale as far as possible, relying on a very restricted and high quality distribution network. Personal objects, clocks and watches, glasses, leather goods, writing materials, perfume, *art de la table*, champagne... the Styling Centre's field of operations takes an eclectic look at life, taking in the everyday as well as the extraordinary, wherever class and creativi- →

ty go hand in hand. Every creation is the result of an autonomous process, fed from a common source of inspiration and capable of leading to a new synthesis of values each time. Only thus can one express from within and not simply through external citations, achieving an unmistakable personality. The product is in fact designed and structured through in-depth research, with the aid of design studies, qualified consultants and workshops for the production of prototypes. It would, however, be wrong to conceive of the Ettore Bugatti marque as a label. The product is not "signed", whatever its nature, but rather the Bugatti marque offers a guarantee of excellence.

EB

The complexity which spreads beyond the design into the construction of the product involves the first hand management of a fundamental aspect: Communication.

Is it possible to communicate a legend? Bugatti is an evocation that makes news with an air of distinction, harmony and class. Far beyond the mere logic of status symbols. For some years now, the sociological studies of consumption have noted a radical transformation of the consumer, especially in the "fashion/luxury" sectors, with a progressive reduction in the standardization of markets.

Some of the objects in the EB range. To the left on the page, L'Art de la Table products. Above, the Bugatti range of cosmetics and in the photo alongside, some of the leather goods. The Bugatti Styling Centre follows each phase from design to production quality control.

Those who intially choose an object to suit their own personal taste feel betrayed when they see the same object forming part of the mass market. In the same way that the value of a status symbol becomes ephemeral once it falls into the hands of all and sundry. Thus an ever greater number of people refusing to become slaves in the service of a banner-

label are recognising that what is in the shop windows today may well be out of fashion by tomorrow. Perhaps the word "fashion" will lose a little of its significance, or perhaps it will assume a contrasting meaning. It would not be the first time such a linguistic transformation has occurred. Is "fashion" on the way out and about to take on the meaning of "bad taste"? It's fashionable, therefore it doesn't last, therefore it's worthless... The era of the all-powerful designer labels is thus over. The ephemeral legends are turning their backs on those who abused them. The Bugatti legend, which is by no means ephemeral, competes in terms of innovation, functionality and respectability under the symbol of

In the photo top, left, the powerful computers in the data processing unit. Top, right, a view of the administration offices. Above, left, Noriko Takeuchi Welponer head of Japanese PR. Right, a view of the stores.

continuity represented by the historic marque. The communication prepared by the Styling Centre for all the licencees (a corporate identity, packaging, product image and point of sale merchandising manual) confirms these concepts through the choice of exclusive codes.

What is there that we could list in memory of the Bugatti legacy? The greater and lesser intuitions of the past... Rembrandt's elephant, Jean's Atlantic, the radiator of the Type 13, the wheel and the filler cap of the Type 35 ...but also the intuitions of the present. First and foremost the very idea that gave rise to Ettore Bugatti. And lastly an extremely "Bugattian" philosophy: excel everywhere. □

The fascinating evolution of the art of cosmetics and scents. Specific recipes for all aspects of beauty care. The functions and propitiatory qualities of the various eccences. Pleasures and refinement through the ages. How the perfumer De Silva has interpreted the Bugatti appeal and style.

CREAMS AND PERFUMES, THOUSANDS OF YEARS OF HISTORY

BY MARIO MERLO

O intments, powders, creams, cosmetics and other similar products date back to the dawn of civilization. As far as we know, they were born in the East and were then diffused throughout the world. There are references that have been found on stone tablets and hieroglyphic inscriptions of ancient origins and, in the case of perfumes, mention is made in the bible, in the Ecclesiastes and in other religious texts, a sign that aromatic preparations had specific functions and important propitiators.

The Phoenicians, Greeks, Etruscans and Romans were all large-scale consumers of scents and perfumes, whilst the classical world is linked to the refinements and abuses of cosmetic art. The art of perfumery

grew, in a certain sense, in the laxity of the most uncertain and indeterminate of all ages from the point of view of virility and courage. Perfumes, in contrast with the first empirical soaps, attracted in all ages not only the approval of women but also of men. It is superfluous to recall that Christianity (contributed to the abatement) of all more or less effeminate habits and pleasures, as well as demonstrations of magnificence and lust, thus also limiting the uses of aromatics and perfumed preparations. The perfumery art reached its splendid zenith with the Romans when all of the refinements of the distant East were absorbed into the city of decadence.

The historians of cosmetics have studied

Above the title, the design of a perfume bottle and its original label from 1845. On the facing page, top, Liane de Pougy, the Femme Fatal at the Casinò de Paris in 1904. Centre, the extremely beautiful Contessa du Barry, a favourite of the King of France. An artistic scent container from ancient Greece.

texts by Teofrasto, Luciano, Antifane, Aspasia, Critone, Galeno, Marco Gavio Apicio and other great names of the classical world, up to Plinius, Ovid and Dioscoride. It is well known that archeological discoveries have often held considerable surprises in this area, bringing to light medicine jars and essences in use in ancient times.

We are not going to search out the magical formulas and the compositions of the perfumes and creams most widely used, but rather we will attempt to illustrate a few of the curiosities regarding the art of perfuming and cleaning oneself for reasons of hygiene or coquetry.

During the Renaissance aromatic essences were very much in favour and the Italian perfumers, already well known even beyond the Alps as ingenious chemists, were considered to be extremely skilled in the technical manipulation of the various ingredients. At the sumptuous courts of the Sforzas, the Medici and the Estensi the passion for perfumes and scents kept pace with the im-

→

moderate ambition of the clothing, particularly cultivated by the Grandes Dames such as Catherine Sforza, Isabella d'Este, Lucrezia Borgia and Catherine de'Medici. It is down to the latter if the Italian recipes penetrated into France to the extent that it became the traditional home of perfumes.

In any case, Italy always held her own, especially in the XVI and XVII centuries when containers of taste and refined workmanship were added to the excellence of the products.

The decline in our production marked the birth and subsequent growth of the industry in Germany, a country where the distillation and distribution of a famous and historic *Eau de Cologne*, invented, as it happens, by an Italian emigrant G. P. Feminis, but later perfected by his relation Gian Maria Farina.

It is well known that Poppaea, wife of the Emperor Nero, passed into history for her extravagant habit of bathing in asses' milk. In order to satisfy this habit no less than five hundred asses had to be sent with her every time she left Rome. Whether it is true or not, the story is reported by Tacitus. The daily immersions and ablutions in the milk probably actually did confer an exceptionally fresh and seductive flesh tone, thanks also to the poultices which she applied day and night. Juvenal severely criticised the vanity of the women of his time which was not even appreciated by their husbands.

Extremely delicate ointments based on Greek grapes, amomum, wine and other rare and expensive balsams of eastern origins are cited; and fourteenth century recipes have been handed down which make use of onion juice, lilies, honey, white wax, bread and milk; musk melon and cucumber waters, musk, chicory, wild camphor, animal marrow, doves and strange vegetable brews: all to be laid up in half pints of wine and to be distiled after laborious treatments.

In fact, historians have noted that Queen Elizabeth of Hungary, who enjoyed a great reputation as a sorceress, claimed to be able to able to "capture youth" through a beauty treatment based on rectified wine spirits, essence of Hungarian rosemary, lemon peel, lemon balm, mint, rose spirit and orange blossom.

Other treatments are cited for "maintaining the face beautiful, softening the hands and making up" based on egg yolks warmed in oil and vigorously blended, the result to be kept in a pot and conserved under a layer of... manure. One could continue citing further rather curious notions, the fruit of the whims of the bewitching Estense and French ladies. We know that Francis I — defeated at the battle of Pavia in 1525 — was particularly susceptible to feminine charms. His court, dominated by Catherine de'Medici, the daughter of Lorenzo the Magnificent and married to the second son of the French king, sparkled for its profusion of parties and beautiful women.

We could add anecdotes and witticisms regarding the fashions for powdered heads, the affectations of the French royals' favourites and the famous "sex symbols" of the sixteenth century, and so on up to the "bella Otero" and the other acclaimed representatives of the "Belle Époque", inventors of the beauty industry; it is here that began the apotheosis of Bugatti, which

In the photo below, the complex but strictly ordered laboratory of a perfume creator. It is the job of these specialists in high perfumery to prepare the new compounds by skilfully blending aromas from all over the world.

A Perfume Mosaic

Bugatti: *a dream-like journey between the appeal of tradition and the promise of the year 2000.*

An itinerary which departs from Grasso, cradle of the perfume industry, and diffuses along a thousand paths before reaching the skyscrapers of Manhattan.

The key to understanding this admirable fragrance is an exhilarating synthesis which combines the style of times gone by, the brio of modernity and the class of a peerless name.

The aromatic tints which confer that background of ever present tradition upon the perfume are typical of Provence (lavender, artemisia and hyssop).

It is initially vivacious, when the classic tones of the neroli and bergamot blend with the fresh aggressiveness of grapefruit and the unusual touch of clementines. All are natural scents which satisfy the ever growing demand for non-artificial perfumes. The heart of the perfume is just as natural and is intended to be the interpre-

tation of the inherent elegance of a Bugatti.

It is distinguished by a cocktail of spices: cloves, nutmeg, coriander and cinnamon.

These are ancient perfumes which join forces with the "head space" essences of jasmine and roses, born out the most advanced technology which allows us to capture their perfume at the moment of greatest splendour.

The base elements gradually make themselves felt to reinforce the character and underline the sensuality of the perfume. Again a mosaic of past, present and future. A parade of vetiver, Russian leather, benzoin and vanilla, along with the modern patchouli and the indispensable presence of musk which contributes to making it a product of the year 2000. Created by Harry Fremont, a native of Grasso who moved to Paris, then Geneva and finally New York where, taking in the past and looking to the future he has interpreted Bugatti. ☐

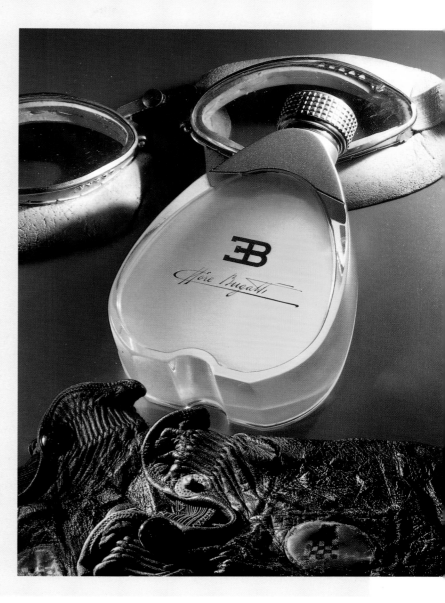

was not only the temple of the most celebrated automobiles, but was also a blend of exclusive and genial discoveries which swept through all walks of life and especially those providing the strongest of emotions.

This could hardly fail to include the scent chosen by the dare-devil artists of the day, the drivers who travelled in clouds of petrol and burnt castor oil vapours mixed with the sweat of physical effort and nervous tension. Today these scents have been updated and adapted to the discretion and class which are the fundamental principles

of the connoisseur of the Bugatti marque.

The committed man, with a life of extremely intense relations and subjected to constant stress, chooses a perfume which gives him that sense of confidence and virility indispensable in the achievement of success. The Bugatti perfume is particularly suitable for accompanying the man throughout his day as it combines three fundamental characteristics: it is refreshing in the morning, it is tenacious and inspires strength during the day and increases in sensuality as night falls. This formidable product has been admirably blended by the great perfumer, Roberto De Silva who already has numerous successes to his name, but who this time has surpassed himself. ☐

THE PRECIOUS WORLD OF CERAMICS

The Ebears firm has produced the fabulous porcelain for the new Ettore Bugatti collection. Splendid dinner services characterized by refined and elegant classic style.

BY ARMIDO CAVALCA

There is a decorative art which in its lightness and apparent fragility has an impassioned feminine beauty: the art of porcelain. Carlo Bugatti had already come into contact with it at the time of his Parisian experiences, proposing an extremely interesting series of pieces for L'Art de la Table. Design and decoration of a mouldable material are activities which are historically associated with the entire Bugatti family. In reproposing, after an interval of many years, a new collection of porcelain carrying the EB name, we are thus grasping a

symbol which forms part of the Bugatti world: love of things of a certain class which play a part in everyday life. Porcelain represents a noble way of approaching food and its correct presentation at the table. Just as it is an inseparable part of an amiable conversation over tea, biscuits and coffee.

Clay, *Kéramos* in Greek from which the word ceramic derives, has been one of the materials most widely used over the centuries, handing down with exquisite inconography epic cycles, bucolic visions, land-
→

*Above the title,
part of the Ebears
firm. Alongside,
the refined, classic
style of the
collection for the
Bugatti Art
de la Table.*

In the two photos alongside, the Bugatti collection is characterized by careful detail design. The exclusive dotted decoration has been produced with extremely sophisticated techniques. On the facing page, the exclusive Bugatti glassware, and a view of Ebears at Annemasse.

scapes and hunting scenes. The Romantic nineteenth century fell in love with this material; its decoration fascinated the avant-garde of the twentieth. The Bugatti legend, which has always involved objects of excellence, could hardly have remained estranged from this appeal. Clay is at the roots of the material: its origins lie beyond the dawn of time: the story of creation speaks of clay, the objects which man made to conserve food and water and to pay homage to his gods and his dead were made of clay.

The working of this material has given rise to whole schools: ceramic materials such as the majolicas (from the ancient name for Majorca in the Balearics) or the faiences from Nevers and Rouen (the name comes from the Italian city of Faenza where this technique was first developed) still provide today precious collectors' objects, as well as being the basis of flourishing industries. The nobility of porcelain stems from the type of mixture and the firing, which renders the surface shiny and translucent. The name derives from the material's similarity to mother-of-pearl shells named *Porcella* by a very famous Venetian, Marco Polo.

It was he who brought Chinese porcelain to Italy in 1271, a porcelain which in that era was enjoying an incomparable artistic splendour. First at Faenza, then in France, Holland, England and Germany, men tried to imitate the Chinese ware: the modern art of ceramics was born. There was a little longer to wait, however, for true porcelain; until the discovery of finer powders, closely

kaolin in the Limoges area. From then on the "Manifactura Royalle" was to grace porcelain with superb style of refined elegance.

What it is that qualitatively differentiates Limoges porcelain, and best of European porcelain, from the faiences and the majolicas is therefore the particularly fine composition of the silico-aluminous mixture and the high firing temperature (900°/1400°) to which it is subjected. This ensures that the material is absolutely safe from attack from external agents. Furthermore, firing at 1400° transforms the kaolin and silicon into a vitreous substance of extraordinary brilliance and translucency.

The substance is mechanically resistant to wide thermal variations. The prized physical and tactile qualities and the wonders of decoration are what cause collectors and dinner guests to catch their breath in admiration.

The class of the porcelain has always mirrored the class of the family which possessed it. Still today, the fineness of the forms, or the choice of colour, lend porcelain a visual quality which for L'Art de la Table is not easily matched. It is actually from these presuppositions of style that the Ettore Bugatti porcelain collection has emerged.

They are splendid table services which combine perfectly the Bugatti principles of style and the precious classicism of the material. The porcelain has been produced by the Ebears firm in Annemasse, which will present the Collection for L'Art de la Table, approved by the Bugatti Styling Centre, throughout the world: a very complete service for the most part dressed in blue and encircled with "gold". Which is no more than it deserves. □

related to the Chinese kaolin.

It was the Germans who were first to discover the powders in the XIII century and maintained the secret for some decades until an Alsatian (a strange geographical coincidence) illegally tried to recover the primary material beyond the Rhine. The French state, under pressure from the aristocracy and the most well off of the Bourgeoisie who boasted extraordinary collections on their estates, had successfully completed research into

GRAND TOUR:
THE SPIRIT OF TRAVEL

*Oreste Franzi, one of the oldest and most famous Italian leather goods
firms, has produced a complete range of products
in collaboration with the Bugatti Styling Centre, dedicated to those who travel*

BY GIUSEPPE MAGHENZANI

On these pages we are offering the history and classic beauty of Grand Tour,
the Ettore Bugatti Collection of leather goods.
It is a story which began in Milan at more
or less the same time as Carlo Bugatti was
about to open that workshop for the decorative arts in wood which was to correctly "instruct" his sons Ettore and Rembrandt.

Whilst Carlo expressed his art in terms of
inlays and parchment, not very far away from
him Rocco Franzi, another worthy Lombard
craftsman, created saddlery, bags and cases
in his workshop near to the Duomo. This
historic concomitance of craft activities
should not be allowed to mislead however:
Ettore decided to follow a different "futurist"
path to that of his father, but in the case of
the Franzis, the tradition begun by Rocco
found willing proselytes in the successive
generations. So much so that to talk about
Grand Tour, we have to trace a path that takes
us from the Bugatti headquarters at Ora to
the Oreste Franzi works at Milan, the firm
which has inherited that nineteenth century
tradition.

Our collection of leather goods, the very
name of which evokes intriguing places and
itineraries, has in fact been entrusted to the
skilled hands of the Milan manufacturers.
The Grand Tour collection, developed by the

Bugatti Styling Centre following a decidedly classical conception of the spirit of travel, is in perfect harmony with the Bugatti tradition and is also executed in a material of
the highest quality. Regarding this aspect
there is also another reference which

→

On the facing page, the Franzi firm's rich medal collection. Above, a "cagna" a traditional leather-working tool.

we are quite happy to cite: Ettore loved leather upholstery. Being such an enthusiast of horses and carriages, he fitted out a department at Molsheim where, rather than extracting horsepower from an engine, he produced exquisite saddlery for his beloved horses.

In Italy there were (and still are) various schools of leather working. For example, a school influenced by the English saddlery tradition grew up at Parma. At Florence, on the other hand, there is a different tradition — as in the Romagna region — which produces fine shoes and bags.

And in Milan a school developed — which in Franzi had one of its masters — which was oriented towards leather travel goods (the famous cases) and small personal articles (wallets etc). The ideal interface between the demands of Ettore Bugatti and the preeminent typology of the Collection has thus found a fertile response in this area of production. The Oreste Franzi company has an exemplary history in the field. Felice, son of Rocco the founder of the dynasty, brought the company to excellent levels of workmanship in the early years of this century.

His personal interpretation of the finish of the product and richness of the hides became known throughout Italy. To the extent that the "Franzi Case", the one supplied to the Royal House of Savoia — or the one sold to the well-off citizens of Milan in the Via Manzoni shop right in the centre of the city — has continued to be a synonym for class

and good taste.

In those early years it was not only the cases which contributed to the firm's reputation: numerous Bugattis and Isotta Fraschinis bore the Franzi name on their interior upholstery. With the third generation, led by Oreste, son of "Cavalier Felice", the company took on international connotations, thanks to a revised structure and a solid commercial and industrial base.

Top, a view of the Franzi works in Via Moneta at Milan as it was some years ago. Below, the firm's logo. On the facing page, the precise finish of the range of Bugatti leather goods.

O. FRANZI & C. sas

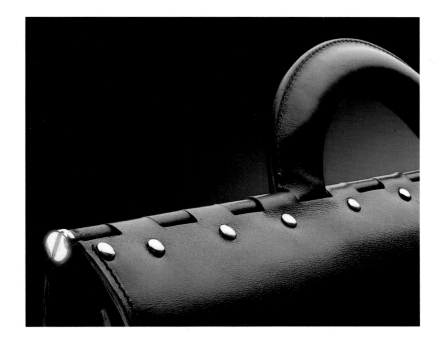

The number of shops increased and production was further diversified with the establishment of new companies (a tannery and a metal foundry) capable of guaranteeing the supply of high quality primary materials and original accessories. The "Compagnia Italiana Isolante" also formed part of this entrepreneurial spirit: it supplied thermos flasks of the necessary quality to Commander Nobile for his expedition to the North Pole. However, the Second World War was a severe blow to Milan and its industrial sectors.

In the immediate post-war period the heirs (the fourth and fifth generations) were faced with a need to understand and respond to industrial production which exploded with the boom of the Sixties. The meeting between the profound experience of the workforce and the new, carefully studied industrial methods produced excellent results.

The links between craft and industry, between ancient and modern, between stylistic distinction and classicism, was rewarded with success. The result of this experience is contained in the Grand Tour.

The Collection is composed of bags and accessories produced with the utmost care to original designs. Travel ideally represents the grand itineraries: from the Renaissance to the Belle Epoque, from the artistic avant-garde of this century to the present day. In the Ettore Bugatti Grand Tour, functionality is also linked to hints of the "mechanical" symbols which have characterized the Bugatti marque: a radiator-like buckle, metal joints that recall rear-view mirror mounting points... and in the folds of the cases, the unmistakable shape of bonnet hinges.

The leather itself, polished outside with nabuk inside, evokes the elegant interiors of the cars of the time. Classic and modern references, aesthetic and functional design, harmony of style and materials: these are the components of the new Grand Tour. □

SOUND SANS FRONTIERES

*Nakamichi, a large Japanese firm specializing in the production
of Hi-Fi components of extremely high quality, has developed an exclusive
and sophisticated audio system for the Bugatti EB 110.*

BY MARCO BELLUCCI

The newly reborn Bugatti stands proudly under the European banner, it is a product of European technological excellence, financed from European sources. Why then was a manufacturer from Japan chosen to contribute? There are not only one but two reasons. First, the fact that Nakamichi's expertise and achievements in the field of car audio were simply not matched by any European manufacturer. But a second, and more important, reason is the Nakamichi attitude towards the art of music, the relentless dedication towards perfect recreation of the musical experience. It is an attitude that leaves no room for compromise, the very same attitude that is embodied by the Bugatti name in the field of automobiles.

One example of this is Nakamichi's concert hall at its Headquarters in Tokyo. The designers and architects went to great lengths to ensure that the acoustics of this hall are on a level with the world's best, to provide a fitting venue for the world's finest performers.

Thus, the Nakamichi concert hall is an environment where dedication to music finds an opportunity to unfold. As such, it has another revealing purpose; for Nakamichi, computers and test instruments are valued tools in the design and production process, but the concert hall is where listening tests and comparisons with live music are carried out.

Nakamichi is justly famous as an innovator in the history of audio. In 1973, the company unveiled the world's first three-head cassette deck, the legendary Model 1000, which opened the way for the cassette as a true high-fidelity medium.

Other celebrated Nakamichi innovations are for example the sophisticated auto-calibration system ABLE (Azimuth, Bias, Level, Equalization), and the NAAC (Nakamichi Auto Azimuth Correction). In
→

In the photo above, Niro Nakamichi, Chairman of the Nakamichi Corporation, alongside Romano Artioli, Chairman of Bugatti Automobili.

Above the Nakamichi concert hall is the most efficient testing instrument for developing audio components technology. Here alongside, the Model 1000, the first three-head analogue cassette deck.

Nakamichi

In the photo alongside, the dashboard of the Bugatti EB 110 with, in the foreground, the control panel of the exceptional Mobile Sound System especially produced by Nakamichi for the Campogalliano Gran Turismo. Bottom, the numerous and complex components which make up the system.

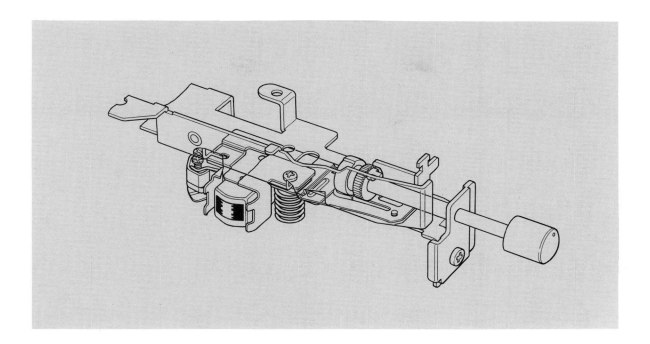

1983, Nakamichi turned its resources and imagination towards another truly challenging field, the world of high-end car audio, with the introduction of a Tuner/Deck that also incorporated this NAAC system, the TD-1200.

Given Nakamichi's impressive credentials, it was obvious that the system chosen for the EB 110 would not be run-of-the-mill. When Nakamichi joined the project, the body shape and chassis design were for the most part completed. But, from the angle of music reproduction, several difficulties emerged, especially regarding speaker placement. Nakamichi engineers explained the crucial importance of exact speaker placement in order to obtain a "live" stereo image in the EB 110.

They performed over 100 acoustical analyses in the interior, determining the crossover point and design, the amplification requirements, and the speaker driver sizes needed. The speaker system was specially developed for the EB 110, employing different cone materials and magnets for compatability with its interior design.

For the sake of musicality, the beautifully finished dashboard had to tolerate holes being cut into it to accomodate the tweeters in their optimum position. Similarly, the door panels were cut in exactly the best spot in which to house the bass/mid drivers. The Nakamichi Tuner/Deck in the center console of the EB 110 features a manual azimuth control that allows fine adjustment of the head to each individual cassette. As an option, a 10-disc CD Changer by Nakamichi can also be installed. This sophisticated piece of equipment delivers a level of performance and sound quality that simply has no equal.

For someone who is a music lover, as well as a connoisseur of fine automobiles, there is no greater luxury than that of listening to this system while driving the EB 110. □

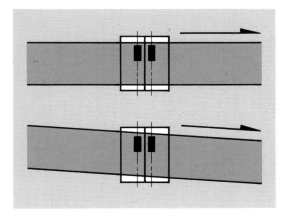

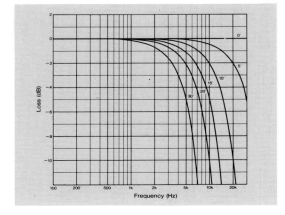

In the drawing above, the layout of the mechanism which adjusts the alignment between the head and the tape. Alongside, in the drawing and the graph, note how a perfect head/tape alignment allows high frequency response to be clearly improved.

Bugattis to race again

It is now official: Bugatti Automobili is to return to motor racing. Its cars will be entered in the competitions valid for the World Championship for Gran Turismo cars. The car destined to inherit the mantle of the legendary sporting Bugattis of the past is the new EB 110 S, lightened and equipped with a 600 hp engine. Bugatti Automobili will

entrust the cars, via the network of concessionaires which it is setting up, to certain Gentleman Drivers able to demonstrate that they are capable of defending the honour of the marque. On the advice of the concessionaires, Bugatti will be happy to offer the best drivers support and assistance.

With the entrance of the EB 110 S, the new Gran Turismo World Championship promises to be highly spectacular, competitive and technologically exciting.

The first deliveries of the EB 110 will take place in October of this year, whilst production of the Supersport is subordinated to the technical specifications to be indicated by the FIA. □

Bugatti international rally

The International Bugatti Rally, organized by the Bugatti Club of France, took place from the 23rd to the 28th of June in the enchanting region occupied by the Chateaux of the Loire. 64 historic Bugattis took part in the event, each different from one another and coming from all over Europe and from the United States. The rally started from the Cistercian Abbey of Epau at Le Mans. The Bugatti enthusiasts, led by Marquis Goulaine, then visited the splendid chateaux scattered throughout the Sarthe, Loire-Atlantique, Maine et Loire and Vendée regions. It was an unforgettable rally in keeping with the Bugatti style and tradition. For the over one hundred participants the exclusive evening at Puy de Fou offered a spectacular open-air event rich in fireworks, scenic attractions and special effects. After the gala evening held at the Epau Abbey, the rally drew to a triumphant conclusion on the Bugatti circuit at Le Mans. □

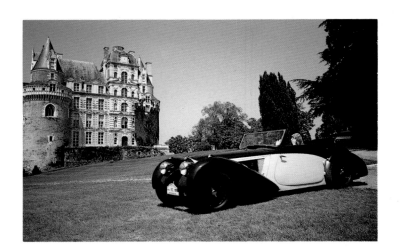

Miniature EB 110

Burago has recently produced and introduced onto the market a splendid 1:18 scale model of the Bugatti EB 110, which is enjoyng great success in the specialist model shops. The perfection of the detailing, the precision of the finish and the elegance of the presentation are the strong suits of the scaled down Bugattis produced by Burago, a company that has consistent-ly offered high quality, faithful reproductions.

The model has upwards opening doors, and opening front and rear bonnets. All the elements of the external structure are cast or pressed in metal. As in the real car, the interior fittings are in light grey whilst the coachwork is finished in classic Bugatti blue.

The features of the EB 110's engine bay and the front compartment are also precisely and faithfully reproduced. The new Bugatti model is certain to arouse the enthusiasm of many collectors.

It is soled with a particularly prestigious natural wood-colour box.

The car is presented on an elegant wooden plinth which lends the model the air of a precious object. □

Bugatti at the Tuscolane villas Festival

Frascati is widely known for the wine produced on its hills overlooking Rome, but less so for its splendid villas. There are around a dozen, all constructed between 1500 and 1600 as summer residences for the noble Roman families.

They contain historical and artistic treasures unknown to many people. An enterprising cultural official has decided to bring these villas back to life, choosing them as the ideal location for theatre, dance concerts and poetry readings.

Thus the "Tuscolane Villas Festival" was born, an event with which Bugatti Automobili is proud to be associated. It is not one of the many festivals which can be visited in Italy on the warm summer evenings, but something special and different. Perhaps because the artistic direction has been entrusted to Pamela Villoresi, an actress of extraordinary charisma, who still believes in real theatre capable of transmitting strong emotions and which does not rely solely on costumes and set designs.

The challenge was by no means easy, but she has had the great courage to contact young actors and contemporary authors from whom she has commissioned new texts, rather than programming classic theatrical works. Herein lies the great novelty of this festival: the return of specially commissioned work as used to be the case in the courts of kings or noble families. Extraordinary plays have come out of this policy, some comic, others dramatic, among which is "Curva Cieca" - "Blind Curve", written by Edoardo Erba on the life of the racing driver Achille Varzi. The Varzi protagonist of a tumultuous existence who sacrificed his career for love, who in the Thirties was a rival of Nuvolari and who often raced in Bugatti cars.

This was one of the motives which encouraged Bugatti Automobili to accept the honour of becoming something of a Patron to the "Tuscolane Villas Festival"; the other motivations have an ethical background. There are many features in common between Bugatti and the organizers of the festival: insistence on dedication, quality and art, enthusiasm and love for what they do and the desire to produce something out of the ordinary. Bugatti produces cars of the ultimate quality with extremely high technological contents; at Frascati a Festival of extremely high cultural standards which has the intention of discovering new talent by offering space to young contemporary playwrights has been organized. This initial experience has been a success which has reinforced this link.

Thus, whilst on the stage at Villa Falconieri the spirit of Achille Varzi was stirring, the new Bugatti "EB 110" listened attentively to a piece of family history... □

Calendar of events 1992

Event	Place	Date
"Art de la Table" fair Presentation of new Bugatti porcelain and crystal glass	Paris September	4-8
Bugatti Festival	Molsheim	11-13 September
Concert and presentation of "EB" accessories	Ora September	15
"Gran Premio" Nuvolari Mantova" Gymkhana for Bugatti cars	Campogalliano September	18-20
Delivery of first cars (EB 110)	Campogalliano	Oct.
Participation of Bugatti Automobili at the World Motor Show -Press days -Gala evening (Vogue magazine) -Public opening	Paris	6-7 Oct. 7 October 8-18 Oct.
"Mipel" leather goods fair Presentation of Bugatti bags and leather goods collection	Milan	16-19 Oct.
"Silmo" glasses fair Presentation of Bugatti glasses collection	Paris	13-15 Nov.
Bologna Motorshow Presentation EB 110 and EB 110 S	Bologna	2-13 Dec.

1993

Event	Place	Date
Geneva international motor show. World debut of new Bugatti model	Geneva	1-14 March
Japan/ Official presentation of Bugatti to the Emperor	Tokyo	April
Mille Miglia Equipe Bugatti technical assistance	Brescia	13-16 May
Rally Bugatti Organized by the Bugatti Club Italia in collaboration with Bugatti Automobili	-	22-23 May

For Information:
EBEARS SA. Avenue Krieg, 44 - CH 1208 Genève
Tel. international code + 22-3465416
Fax 22-3476397

REFINED ART DE LA TABLE

The EB Ettore Bugatti L'Art de la Table collection has been produced by Ebears, a company which boasts a long tradition in the production of objects of artistic quality. The basic form of the Collection, which will be distributed in an extremely restricted chain of sales points from next autumn, has been defined by the Bugatti Styling Centre, guaranteeing absolute stylistic coherency. The use of the precious decorative art of porcelain, which in Limoges has one of its most important centres from the cultural and historical points of view, takes its place in the Bugatti world with a a project rich in classical references. It could hardly be otherwise: the Collection has as its dominant motifs - both on the single plates as well as the complete services - blue, "Pompei" red and gold. These colours, combined with the quality of the supporting materials, demonstrate a historical continuity not only with the Bugatti Marque, but also with the most noble traditions of L'Art de la Table.

A RETURN TO WRITING

The Bugatti legend has always been able to combine the modernity of intuition with classicism. When it comes to pens, which represent a sign of distinctions in "provate" writing, the Bugatti Styling Centre has therefore opted for a solution which priviliges a both the beauty of aesthetics and precision functioning of mechanisms. The Collection devoted to "beautiful calligraphy" is directly distributed by Ettore Bugatti at Ora.

TRAVEL AND BUSINESS: UNITED BY STILE

The Collection of Leather goods, approved by the Bugatti Styling Centre and distributed by the old-established manufacturer Franzi of Milan, brings together a series of objects suitable not only for travelling in style, but also for those important business meetings.

The Collection proposes a complete vision of the modern man through the stylistic revisiting of "small leather goods" (wallets, portfolios etc) and classic travel luggage.

For information:
ETTORE BUGATTI S.r.l., Via Nazionale, 75
I-39040 Ora (Bolzano)
Tel. international code + 471-816111
Fax 471-816222

THE ESSENCE OF A PERFUME

At the international presentation of the Bugatti Perfume, which took place last April, the importance of an "essence" around the legend was underlined. The successful work on the styling of the packaging and the careful choice of the essences by the De Silva laboratories, are today combined a full range of products for men: Eau de Toilette, After shave, Bath Foam, Eau de Cologne, Deodorant Spray and Braonzing Gel.

For information:
DE SILVA COSMETIQUE
Via Castelli Fiorenza, 33/37
I-20017 RHO (MI)
Tel. international code + 2-93338219
Fax 2-9304866

A NOBLE TOAST

Ettore Bugatti Champagne is born of a noble lineage: La Maison de Castellane. Situated at Epernay, the firm — created by the Viscount Florens de Castellane in 1895 — boasts an d exceptional patrimony: almost 10 km of "cave". The Ettore Bugatti Champagne is "Millesimée" and is the result of a perfect marriage of Chardonnay "Crus" and Pinot Nero, with all the grapes coming from the excellent 1982 harvest.

For information:
DE CASTELLANE, 57 Rue de Verdun
F-51204 Epernay Cedex
Tel. int. code + 26551533
Fax 26542481

The EB Ettore Bugatti marque offers a complete desktop writing set, produced and distributed directly by Ettore Bugatti.

For information:
ETTORE BUGATTI S.r.l., Via Nazionale, 75
I-39040 Ora (Bolzano)
Tel. international code + 471-816111 - Fax 471-816222

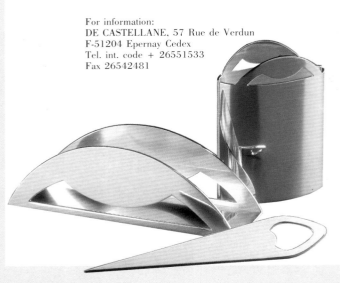

NEW BUGATTI EB110
by BBURAGO

1/18

DIE-CAST METAL MODEL 1:18 DIAMONDS
cod. 3035
BUGATTI EB 110 (1991)

La grande epopea della Casa di Molsheim

In un prezioso, esclusivo volume tutta la storia dei capolavori Bugatti

Hugh Conway e Maurice Sauzay, due grandi storici dell'automobile, hanno condensato in una opera di 560 pagine più di trent'anni di accurate ricerche condotte sulle vicende umane e imprenditoriali della Casa automobilistica creata dal genio tecnico e artistico di Ettore Bugatti. Grazie alla collaborazione di Musei, istituzioni culturali e collezionisti privati è stato possibile raccogliere nel prestigioso volume Bugatti Magnum della Giorgio Nada Editore una incredibile quantità di documenti e fotografie di notevole interesse storico. Un libro unico, completo e definitivo che non può mancare nella biblioteca di ogni autentico appassionato. L'edizione, a tiratura limitata e numerata, è racchiusa in un prestigioso cofanetto rifinito come la classica lamiera zincata tipica delle mitiche Bugatti.

GIORGIO NADA EDITORE